Building an Academic Community

The Middle School Teacher's Guide to the First Four Weeks of the School Year

From **Responsive Classroom**®
with Ellie Cornecelli and Amber Searles

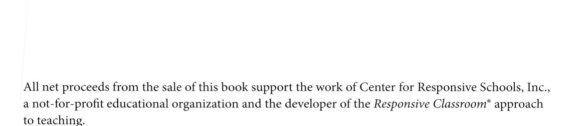

All net proceeds from the sale of this book support the work of Center for Responsive Schools, Inc., a not-for-profit educational organization and the developer of the *Responsive Classroom*® approach to teaching.

Many of the stories in this book are based on real events. To respect students' privacy, names and identifying characteristics of the students and situations have been changed.

ISBN: 978-1-892989-92-5
Library of Congress Control Number: 2018958604

Classroom photographs by Jeff Woodward, except where noted

Center for Responsive Schools, Inc.
85 Avenue A, P.O. Box 718
Turners Falls, MA 01376-0718

800-360-6332
www.responsiveclassroom.org

Second printing 2019

Contents

Introduction

The beautiful thing about learning is nobody can take it away from you.

—B. B. King, musician

Imagine the beginning of the school year. Students, still buzzing with energy from summer vacation, are laughing and talking with one another. There's a sense of anticipation as they get ready to start a new grade, learn from new teachers, and meet new classmates. It's a time of fresh opportunity for teachers, too, as we anticipate greeting our classes and getting the school year off to a great start.

Now imagine harnessing all of this beginning-of-the-year energy and using it as a springboard for an engaged and productive school year, built on the solid foundation established during the first few weeks of school. The techniques, tools, and strategies in this book will show you how to bring this vision to life.

The *Responsive Classroom* Approach—Safe, Joyful, and Engaging

Responsive Classroom is an evidence-based education approach associated with greater teacher effectiveness, higher student achievement, and improved school climate. The approach was developed by a group of public school educators who had a vision of bringing together social and academic learning throughout the school day.

The *Responsive Classroom* approach consists of a set of practices that build academic and social-emotional skills and that can be used along with many other programs. The approach helps educators build competencies in four interrelated domains:

- **Engaging academics**—Designing and delivering high-quality, rigorous, and engaging instruction

- **Positive community**—Creating a safe, predictable, joyful, and inclusive classroom, where all students have a sense of belonging and significance

- **Effective management**—Creating a calm, orderly environment that promotes autonomy and allows students to focus on learning

- **Developmentally responsive teaching**—Responding to students' individual, cultural, and developmental learning needs and strengths

The strategies and ideas in the chapters that follow will help you build the skills needed to create a safe and engaging classroom and school where all students feel a sense of belonging and significance.

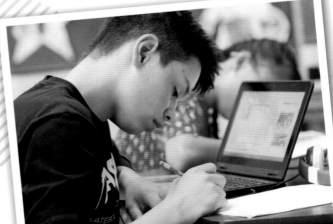

The First Four Weeks

Whether students are new to the school or have been there for years, and whether class-mates are meeting for the first time or have known one another since kindergarten, each new school year presents a fresh start. Every class is composed of a unique group of students, with their own needs and at varying stages of development. This means that each fall, we need to start anew in building a strong foundation for learning.

This foundation will give students the tools and solid grounding they need in order to succeed as members of the classroom community. Students need a firm grasp of the rules and an understanding of procedures and routines, as well as a sense of belonging that allows them to feel safe taking academic risks. In this book, you'll find tips and techniques for positive classroom management and discipline, classroom community building, and other ways to create conditions in which students can be successful.

A Fresh Start Anytime

The beginning of the school year is just one possible starting point. You can adapt the plans and strategies in this book to use at the beginning of a new quarter or semester, or if you're a new teacher joining an established classroom. You may find them helpful partway through the year if you sense that students need a fresh start in building a stronger classroom community. Use the full four-week plan or choose the ideas that will best support your class in the areas where additional teaching and practice are most needed.

Getting the Most From This Book

This book divides the first four weeks of school into five periods:

- The First Day of School

- The Rest of Week One

- Week Two

- Week Three

- Week Four

The chapter for each period begins with a brief overview and a set of goals for that period. The strategies for achieving these goals are organized in three sections:

- **Creating Conditions for Success** includes key routines, procedures, and tips for use in the classroom, during Advisory, in the hallway and cafeteria, during transitional times, and at the end of the day.

- **Teaching Academics** helps you design and deliver engaging academics and helps students develop an academic mindset and build essential skills.

- **Teaching Discipline** shows you how to employ healthy, effective discipline practices and respond to misbehavior in productive ways in order to create a safe environment for learning.

The following concepts and practices are tools to use in your interactions with students in all three of these areas, and are incorporated in the ideas and strategies discussed throughout this book.

Teacher Language

The language you use when addressing students is one of the most powerful tools you have as a teacher. Your tone and choice of words can let students know you believe in them and their ability to behave well and succeed academically. Effective teacher language conveys faith in students' good intentions, and it focuses on actions rather than being personal.

Throughout this book, you'll see references to several different types of teacher language.

- **Envisioning language** helps students see a path to their own potential. By referring to students as "scientists," "writers," or "active citizens," you can help them shape their identity around having the ability to reach these goals. You can also use envisioning language at the start of a lesson or unit of study to help students visualize what a successful outcome will look like: "This month, you're going to research historical figures who influenced the technology we use today, and you'll become an expert on one of these people for your final presentation."

- **Reinforcing language** lets students know—and build on—what they're doing well. Reinforcing language should be specific and factual. Rather than simply saying "Good job," try "You really listened carefully to your partner" or "The way you explained your ideas in your essay shows you've been working hard on making your writing persuasive."

- **Reminding language** prompts students to remember expectations they've learned and to make positive decisions based on those expectations. It can help students get back on task if they've started to head in the wrong direction ("What should you be working on right now?") and can also be used proactively before a potential challenge to keep students focused ("What are some guidelines to remember as you choose teams for volleyball?").

- **Redirecting language** is used when a student has gotten fully off task and needs help refocusing. Redirecting language consists of direct, specific, and nonnegotiable statements. It should be delivered in a neutral but firm tone and identify what the student should do immediately: "Alex, put the markers down and join your writing workshop group." Because middle school students are highly conscious of how their peers perceive them, try to keep your redirections as quiet as possible so that only the individual student can hear them.

A few general guidelines help shape the use of teacher language. First, assume that students have positive intentions. If you maintain the belief that they want to learn, get along with others, and succeed, you'll be in a better position to help them do all those things. Second, remember that mistakes—both academic and behavioral—are part of learning. Address mistakes in a kind, matter-of-fact way, and be sure to speak to all students in this same caring manner. Finally, keep your own talk to a minimum to allow space for students to think and express themselves, and to give your own words more impact.

To learn more about teacher language, see *The Power of Our Words for Middle School: Teacher Language That Helps Students Learn* (Center for Responsive Schools, 2016).

Open-Ended Questions

A powerful strategy for engaging students and letting them know that their ideas matter is asking open-ended questions. Ideal for discussing both academic and social-emotional matters, these questions allow students to expand their thinking, and help you assess students' understanding. Open-ended questions have no right or wrong answers, instead letting students provide any reasoned, relevant responses they can come up with: "What are some ways you might see Newton's First Law of Motion in action around school?" Open-ended questions should convey your genuine curiosity to hear students' thoughts and inspire cooperation rather than competition among students.

Interactive Modeling

Although middle school students have been in school for years, it's important not to assume they'll know how to follow every routine in your classroom. Some students may need additional practice in the basics. Plus, every classroom is different—it may have been fine with a previous teacher for students to get up and sharpen their pencils during instruction, but you might prefer that they use an already sharpened pencil from a communal supply to avoid disruption. Be clear about your expectations, and be sure to teach the procedures you need students to follow.

One effective way to teach all kinds of classroom procedures is Interactive Modeling. This four-step process helps students understand, practice, and remember skills and procedures. Here's an example of how you could use Interactive Modeling to teach students how to handle a piece of lab equipment.

1. **Describe what you will model and why.** Provide a clear statement to help students focus: "We're about to begin our unit on chemistry. We'll be using glass beakers, so I'm going to show you how to handle them safely."

2. **Model while students notice.** Demonstrate the skill or routine without narrating what you're doing. For example, you might pick up the beaker using both hands, walk carefully across the room, and place it down gently in the middle of a lab table. Give students the chance to observe you for themselves. Afterward, ask them what they noticed.

3. **Give students the opportunity to collaborate and practice.** While your demonstration is fresh in their minds, allow students to practice the skill and cement the steps in their minds.

4. **Reinforce their practice with immediate feedback.** State the specific positive actions you saw students take, and respectfully correct any mistakes you observed: "I saw people holding beakers with both hands to carry them. I also saw everyone gently placing their beakers on the table."

In addition to teaching classroom procedures, Interactive Modeling can be used to teach academic skills, such as finding the area of a triangle, as well as social-emotional skills, such as disagreeing respectfully. Although Interactive Modeling is typically done without narrating what you're doing, some skills require students to understand a particular thought process. In these cases, you can use the think-aloud technique to make your thinking apparent. You might choose to have a visible signal for think-alouds, such as holding a finger to your head, or you might simply tell students that you're going to do a think-aloud to model a particular skill. For example, during step two of modeling how to give constructive criticism in a writing workshop, you might say, "Hmm, I can't really picture what's going on except for what the character looks like. I don't know anything about the setting. I'll start with the positive and suggest that she build on that: 'I have a clear picture of the character, and I'd also like to know what the place looks like. Maybe you could add more details to the description of the setting.'"

Responsive Advisory Meeting

During the middle school years, students are especially in need of strong relationships with trusted adults. An Advisory program provides students with opportunities to form this kind of relationship, as well as to build healthy connections with other students and a good sense of community.

Responsive Advisory Meeting, a key *Responsive Classroom* middle school practice, helps you make the most of Advisory time through a well-organized, purposeful meeting structure. This structure is designed to support students academically and bolster their social-emotional learning while meeting their developmental needs for belonging, significance, and fun.

Responsive Advisory Meeting consists of four components, each of which plays an important role in achieving the goals of Advisory.

- **Arrival welcome**—As students enter the classroom, the teacher offers a friendly greeting and welcomes each one by name.

- **Announcements**—In advance, the teacher writes a message on the board or another location where all students can see it. The message includes thought starters for the meeting, as well as any upcoming events and other information about the life of the school.

- **Acknowledgments**—Students form pairs or small groups and share responses to a prompt in the announcements message or another question the teacher poses.

- **Activity**—The whole group does an activity related to the purpose of the meeting.

Each meeting concludes with a question designed to help students reflect on that meeting's purpose and content.

A complete Responsive Advisory Meeting as outlined above should generally take about 20 minutes and is ideally done at the same time on most or all days of the week. However, if your school does not have a specific time for Advisory in the schedule, you can adapt your meetings to fit in before class or during part of homeroom, allowing students to experience many of the benefits Responsive Advisory Meeting can provide. You might also choose to begin all classes with an arrival welcome and announcements message in order to get each period off to a good start.

In this book, you'll find tips and ideas to help you create Responsive Advisory Meeting plans for each of the first four weeks of school. For additional meeting plan ideas, see *The Responsive Advisory Meeting Book: 150+ Purposeful Plans for Middle School* (Center for Responsive Schools, 2018).

Interactive Learning Structures

Interactive learning structures are lively, easy-to-use activities that enable students to engage more deeply with their learning by moving around, stretching their thinking, and positively interacting with their peers. While these activities are enjoyable for students to do, they are also purposeful structures designed to help students strengthen their academic and social-emotional skills. By meeting young adolescents' developmental needs for learning that's both experiential and social, interactive learning structures motivate students to stay on task, foster a strong classroom community, and encourage maximum effort.

Each structure helps you quickly organize students into pairs or small groups and provides a format that allows students to work together on a specific learning goal, assignment, or project. At the very beginning of the year, when students are just starting to get to know one another, rely on simpler activities that present less of an academic and social risk. Later on, when students are more comfortable in the classroom community, you can introduce higher-risk activities, such as those that involve larger groups or presentations in front of the class.

In addition to the interactive learning structures presented in this book, you can find other ideas in *Middle School Motivators! 22 Interactive Learning Structures* (Center for Responsive Schools, 2016).

Brain Breaks

Brain breaks are quick whole-class activities that give students a break from rigorous academics. They can be used either to bring students' energy up, such as during an afternoon slump or after a lengthy test, or to help students achieve a more peaceful or calm state, such as after an assembly or a class disruption. Brain breaks address a variety of young adolescents' needs:

- **Social-emotional needs**—Middle school students have a strong interest in being with and learning from their peers. Brain breaks offer structured ways to support healthy interactions between students, allowing them to develop the social-emotional skills they need to master rigorous academics in the intensely social context of middle school.

- **Cognitive needs**—In addition to building critical-thinking skills as students form mental pictures, make quick decisions, and follow motion or word patterns, brain breaks have a physiological basis for promoting cognitive development. The movement involved in each brain break sends oxygen and nutrients to the brain, stimulating brain cells and supporting students' mood, memory, and motivation.

- **Physical needs**—These opportunities for safe movement can also help students release excess energy and relieve physical tension during this time of rapid development.

Brain breaks are versatile and easy to incorporate throughout the school day, at any time during a class period. As with interactive learning structures, look for lower-risk activities at the beginning of the year, then gradually move toward higher-risk activities as students become more comfortable with one another.

Look for brain break ideas throughout this book, as well as in *Refocus and Recharge! 50 Brain Breaks for Middle Schoolers* (Center for Responsive Schools, 2016).

Active Teaching

The learning process occurs in a natural cycle, whether one is learning new academic content or learning a new hobby. Active teaching supports students throughout this cycle, which is composed of three stages.

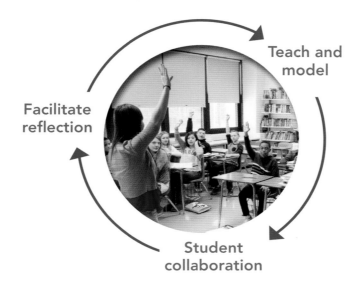

- **Teach and model**—The learning cycle begins with a sense of purpose. When introducing a new topic of study, encourage students to think about what they would like to learn in this unit, what they already know, and what goals they can set for themselves.

- **Student collaboration**—Next comes a period of exploration as students work together to explore, experiment, gather information, try out new skills, and follow their curiosity to learn more. Rather than giving instruction that only allows students to watch and listen, invite them to investigate new ideas and solve problems on their own.

- **Facilitate reflection**—Guide students as they assess what they discovered, what did or didn't work, and what ideas they might wish to explore further. This stage allows students to incorporate new knowledge into their understanding of the world and set new goals as the cycle begins again.

Building your lesson plans around this natural cycle can help you create lessons that maximize student interest, engagement, and thinking. You'll learn more about the complete process of active teaching in week three.

Teaching Discipline

Just like math, social studies, or any other subject, discipline can be taught. Rather than simply telling students the rules and then enforcing them, the process of teaching discipline is meant to help students develop their own intrinsic motivation to follow the rules. Teaching discipline is essential to establishing and maintaining a safe, predictable classroom where all students can practice self-control, do their best learning, and have a sense of belonging and significance. This work begins on the first day of school and continues all year long.

Effective discipline practices include both proactive strategies (teaching students how to follow the rules) and reactive strategies (helping students get back on task if they do not follow the rules). The majority are proactive and require up-front time and effort, but teachers who put in this effort experience less off-task behavior and misbehavior. These practices are neither punitive nor permissive; instead, they are kind yet firm. They work because they help to develop mutually respectful teacher-student and student-student relationships and create a strong sense of community, where students can learn effectively.

Over the first four weeks of school, this book will walk you through the process of helping students set goals, connect those goals to the rules, and become invested in the rules as a way of helping them achieve their goals. You'll also learn strategies for keeping the rules alive and responding to misbehavior that you can carry throughout the year.

The Benefits of a Strong Foundation for the Year

Think about what your ideal classroom might look like later on in the year. Maybe you envision students thoughtfully working together in writing workshop or art critique groups. Perhaps you picture them safely and carefully doing science experiments or new physical education activities. No matter what subjects you teach, the tools in this book can help you achieve your educational goals and fulfill your vision for the school year.

By helping students understand and follow rules and routines, form positive relationships with one another and with you, and actively engage with learning, you're giving them the tools they need to stay motivated and achieve success.

Preparing for the School Year

As a classroom community, our capacity to generate excitement is deeply affected by our interest in one another, in hearing one another's voices, in recognizing one another's presence.

—bell hooks, author and social activist

A successful start to the school year begins with preparation. In this chapter, you'll find ways to begin forming productive relationships with students, communicate with families, get the classroom ready, and find the support you need to sustain momentum as the school year gets going.

Getting to Know Students

Students feel a stronger sense of belonging and are more invested in classroom life when their teachers know them as individuals, and this process can begin even before the first day of school. Here are a few ideas to help you get to know the students you'll be teaching.

Check In With Last Year's Teachers

Previous teachers can provide a wealth of information about students' academic strengths and challenges. You might learn about students' likes and interests, helping you build connections with them right away. Previous teachers can also offer advice on any behavioral or personal issues students may be facing, and may have good ideas for connecting with these students, dealing with behavior issues, and avoiding outburst triggers.

Review Student Records

Report cards, test scores, reading levels, and attendance records can offer insights into many aspects of students' school histories. For example, did a student do well on their report card but struggle on standardized tests? Consider also what you've learned from talking with last year's teachers—did a student's grades dip after a difficult family event or during a particular social challenge at school?

Talk to Other School Personnel

Consult with school counselors, administrators, school nurses, and special education teachers to learn about incoming students' needs. Build the groundwork now so that you can stay in communication throughout the year about how students are doing and get any help you might need.

Connect at Back-to-School Events and Open Houses

Back-to-school nights and similar events give students and their families the opportunity to meet their new teachers, and give you the chance to start getting to know incoming students. Ask each student their name (making a note of any pronunciation you'll need to practice), let them know some of the exciting things you'll be teaching this year, and ask what they are interested in learning about. Pay attention to whether they seem excited to get started or might need a bit more encouragement to feel comfortable as the year begins.

Consider Students' Developmental Stages

Even if you've taught a student in previous years, the rapid changes of adolescence can make them behave very differently from year to year. A student who's an impulsive, goofy sixth grader might develop into a steadier, more confident seventh grader and then a sensitive, quiet eighth grader. Any given class will likely represent a range of developmental stages, as students at any age progress through these stages at different rates. Understanding students developmentally is one of the key elements of knowing them as individuals and is crucial to helping them learn effectively.

To learn more about child and adolescent development and how it relates to life in the classroom, see *Yardsticks: Child and Adolescent Development Ages 4–14,* 4th edition, by Chip Wood (Center for Responsive Schools, 2017).

Communicating With Parents*

Connecting with parents toward the end of the summer helps lay the groundwork for a fruitful year of collaboration. When you make the effort to get to know and communicate with parents, you become a more effective teacher for their children. It's easier to share information with them, and they're more likely to do the same with you. And the more you know about students' families and home

lives, the better you can support their growth and meet their needs. Consider these suggestions for starting to build a productive relationship with parents.

Send a Message

A few weeks before school starts, consider sending a friendly letter or email to parents to introduce yourself and generate a sense of warmth and trust. This communication is also an opportunity to share a few tips for helping students get ready for the first day of school.

Host an Open House or Meet-and-Greet

It's helpful to give families the opportunity to meet you in person to introduce themselves and check out your classroom and the school. Let them know when you'll be available to have them come by your classroom and say hello. If you are part of a team of teachers, you could work together to organize an open house, where students and families can come and meet all the teachers on the team.

Stay Connected

Keeping the lines of communication open with parents is an important way of supporting students' success. Here are some ideas for staying in touch with parents throughout the school year:

- Create a classroom or team website. Use it to share news about what's happening in the classroom and school and to provide an easy way for parents to contact you.

- Send a monthly digital newsletter to parents to showcase what students are working on.

- Organize a regular community event, such as a quarterly open house, to highlight students' work and the content you teach. You could team up with other teachers to enrich the event.

- Find ways to connect the skills students are building in your classroom to their lives outside school. For example, if students are learning about archaeology, you could invite a local historian to come in and talk about findings from archaeological studies that have been done in your area. Invite parents to these events so they, too, can see the relevance of what students are learning.

- Use a blog or social media to let parents and others in the school community follow the progress of particular experiments or projects in your classroom.

- Invite accomplished professionals in the field of your subject area to speak at the school, and invite parents to attend. Successful artists, engineers, musicians, athletes, and pioneers in technology or business can be an inspiring way to show how your subject area can lead to possible future career tracks.

Preparing the Classroom (and Beyond)

Help students feel comfortable and ready to start the work of learning and building a classroom community by setting up your space for success. Here are some tips to help you make your classroom an inviting, lively, and well-organized place to learn.

Furniture

Consider what type and arrangement of furniture will best promote learning in your classroom. Tables or desks arranged in clusters of around four are an excellent layout for facilitating small group work. In some schools, flexible seating may be an option— a mix of traditional desks, standing tables or desks, sofas, or other types of work areas that support a variety of different learning styles. With any furniture arrangement, you might choose to assign seats to relieve any anxiety students are feeling about where and with whom to sit, at least in the early part of the year. Having students create name tags or cards can be a good first-day icebreaker and a way to help everyone learn each other's names.

Décor

Keep posters, charts, and other decorations minimal at the start of the year. A well-organized classroom with plenty of space available shows students that there's room for their input and their work. You might decide to display a few posters related to the subject matter you'll be teaching early on or reference charts that will apply throughout the year. You might also place labels at the top of otherwise empty bulletin boards to show students where their work will be displayed as the year goes on.

Supplies and Equipment

Keep supplies that will be used early and often in clearly marked and well-organized containers or shelves for students to access. It can help you keep things running smoothly to have some frequently used supplies, such as pencils and rulers, in a box or caddy at each table cluster. Materials or equipment that will be introduced later may be kept out of

sight in closed cabinets, or you could build excitement by putting "Coming Attraction!" or "Sneak Preview!" signs on them. Later, when you've introduced how to properly use these items, you can store them in areas that allow students to access them as needed.

Beyond the Classroom

With your teammates or other teachers or administrators, brainstorm ways to maintain consistency between nonclassroom spaces and the environment you want to create in your classroom. You might think about hanging signs or posters in hallways and the cafeteria to promote positive community and remind students of rules and routines.

Working With Your Team

Before the school year starts, get together with the members of your teaching team to plan how you'll create a consistent and positive learning environment for all students on the team. (If you do not have an assigned team, consider creating your own team with other teachers—for example, a team of exploratory teachers.) As noted in previous sections, it can be effective to work with your teammates on planning student and family outreach, such as open houses, and on creating consistency between classrooms. Here are some additional suggestions for working with your team before the year begins.

Modeling Skills for Success

Discuss together which procedures and academic or social-emotional skills need to be taught on day one or during the first week of school. Brainstorm a list of skills to teach through Interactive Modeling (see pages 6–7), such as:

- Entering the classroom

- Signing out a hall pass

- Active listening

- Disagreeing respectfully

- Handling supplies and equipment

Think about how to divide these topics between teachers so that students don't hear the same instructions repeatedly and tune out as a result. For example, you might decide that the science teacher will model how to partner up at tables, while the math teacher will model active listening. By spreading these lessons across class periods, you'll also help ensure that no one teacher winds up spending the entire first day teaching basic procedures, and that everyone has a chance to start teaching their own content.

In addition, make sure that you delegate who will teach various procedures for spaces outside the classroom and transitional times so that these important expectations don't fall through the cracks. Make a plan with your colleagues to model procedures that students need to follow when changing classes, going to their lockers, waiting in the lunch line, or heading to the buses at the end of the day.

Create Common Expectations for Behavior

Students will have a better understanding of how they're expected to behave—and they'll know those expectations will be enforced—if all teachers on the team are in alignment about behavior. As a group, discuss what the rules will be, what they will look like in action, and how you will respond when the rules get broken.

Effective rules frame an ideal and are presented as positive statements, meant to guide students toward a desired behavior rather than away from an undesired one. By stating rules this way, you can help students envision and work toward a positive classroom and school community. Rules should also be global in nature so that they can be applied to a broad range of situations in school and so that students can practice reasoned, critical, and ethical thinking as they figure out how to apply those rules.

Three to five rules are enough to cover just about every situation while still being easy for students to remember. Consider a list including rules that touch on these categories:

- Taking care of and respecting oneself
- Taking care of and respecting others
- Taking care of and respecting school spaces and materials
- Doing one's best work

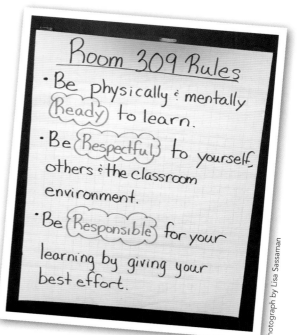

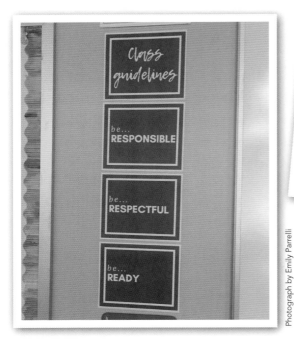

Photograph by Lisa Sassaman

Photograph by Emily Parrelli

After you've created a set of team rules (or have discussed how to implement schoolwide rules within your team), think about ways to communicate your consensus about behavior to students, such as:

- A catchy team phrase or slogan that can be displayed in classrooms and hallways

- A collage of photos of all staff members on the team to show unity

- Meetings with all teachers and students on the team to help build a sense of community, give all students the same messages about expectations, and allow students to ask questions and speak out about concerns

Connecting Academic Content

Talk with your colleagues about ways to help students relate the content of your class with their other classes. Each teacher on the team might bring their syllabus to compare before the year starts, and the team could brainstorm connections between subjects. For example, a science unit about soundwaves might be enhanced by connecting with content in a music class. Or, a math unit about the Pythagorean theorem might relate to a history unit

about ancient Greece. By highlighting these connections from the beginning of the year—and perhaps even co-teaching some lessons—you can enhance students' understanding of what they're learning and help them see the ways academic content connects to the world at large.

Elective and exploratory teachers may want to work together to set cohesive norms and procedures for the first day. It may be useful to discuss:

- How you will communicate the importance of your content to students

- Ways to illustrate to students and parents the skills students will practice in your class

- How your content areas can come together to showcase the work you do

- How you could collaborate with other teachers in the grade level to support cross-content learning

Teacher Self-Care

Teaching can bring great joy and satisfaction, but any teacher knows that it also takes a lot of mental and emotional energy. In order to stay engaged with students and—most importantly—to maintain your physical and emotional health, it's essential to practice good self-care.

As the school year begins, it's easy to get caught up in work, not to mention family responsibilities and other obligations. Before the year starts, take some time to relax and to get into routines for self-care that you can carry throughout the year. Now might be a good time to sign up for an exercise class, set a weekly or monthly coffee date with a friend, or get into the habit of meditating for a few minutes each day.

Now is also a good time to strengthen your connections with other educators in your school community. Just as students need to have a sense of belonging, so do you! Plan regular times to get together with colleagues to brainstorm solutions to challenges that may come up. Ask for help when you need it from teammates or other teachers, administrators, and other school personnel. You might even consider an occasional after-work get-together, where you and your colleagues can blow off some steam, bond, and recharge. In week four, you'll find additional ideas to help carry you through the rest of the school year.

The First Day of School

You have to go wholeheartedly into anything in order to achieve anything worth having.

—Frank Lloyd Wright, architect

This chapter provides a range of ideas and tips to serve as a starting point as you plan for one of the most important days of the school year. Ideally, the first day will be well organized and calm, with a sense of positive energy, and it will set a tone of high expectations and send a message to students that they are welcomed and valued.

As you begin to envision this first day, think about where students are developmentally. Young adolescents are in a transitional stage. As they grow physically, they are also developing socially, emotionally, and cognitively. It is typical for students at this age to try on new identities and show passion for their ideas as they establish their independence. Yet, adolescence can also be a time of paradox. Students still need strong connections with adults, but as they strive for independence, they may distance themselves from parents and teachers. They may show great responsibility with certain assignments while putting off smaller tasks that they view as unimportant.

Teaching adolescents can be deeply rewarding as you watch students develop new cognitive skills, such as abstract reasoning. It can also be challenging as students test boundaries and assert their independence. Middle school educators must find a balance between helping students succeed in the structured environment of school and encouraging them to develop their own unique interests and personalities.

Goals for Day One

Students can feel excited, curious, and a little anxious as the new school year approaches. While looking forward to reconnecting with friends and getting back to some familiar routines, they may also worry about adapting to new classes and meeting new challenges. Teachers, too, may feel a mix of emotions at the beginning of a new year. Changes in school staff, schedules, or lesson plans may require you to adjust, sometimes at the last minute. But these challenges offer an opportunity to empathize with students. They have to adapt, too—to new teachers, new environments, the changes of adolescence, and other shifts outside their control. You can set a good example as you model positive ways to handle any changes that arise.

The goals for the first day of school are intended to help you start building the foundation for a rewarding school year.

1. **Help students start building a sense of belonging and significance.** Every student needs to understand that they are a valued member of the classroom community. Having a sense of belonging (being part of a group) and significance (being known as an individual) helps them build this community of learners.

2. **Communicate a vision of students as capable learners.** By clearly communicating class expectations—and expressing your belief that students can meet them—you help students become responsible, self-motivated learners. Support them by modeling important behaviors and skills and offering plenty of opportunities to practice.

3. **Build a sense of competence about the academic work ahead.** Start the first day of school with active and interactive learning experiences that will get students excited about upcoming academic content, and show them that they're capable of doing the challenging and engaging work that lies ahead.

4. **Introduce the rules, and calmly redirect misbehavior.** When introducing the rules, emphasize to students that the rules are in place to foster success, collaboration, accountability, and safety. Using a calm, neutral tone and body language, promptly redirect any behavior that is on its way to becoming misbehavior. Demonstrate to students that this redirection is nonnegotiable but that you trust them to respond with an immediate change in behavior.

Creating Conditions for Success

Students want to be successful in school. It's important for teachers to hold this as a universal truth, and the first day of school is a prime opportunity to communicate this belief to all the students you teach. Whether a student is fresh out of elementary school or it's the beginning of their last year before they transition to high school, the first day of school should feel orderly, welcoming, and responsive. Creating such an atmosphere will go a long way toward helping students feel the sense of belonging and significance that is critical to their academic, social, and emotional development.

Building Community

Positive community in a school and a classroom begins with students feeling a sense of belonging and significance. Think of some things you can do to foster these feelings on the first day of school for every student in the classroom community. What sort of initial encounter between you and students (and between students and their peers) will lay the foundation for a community that demonstrates the skills of cooperation, assertiveness, and empathy? Here are some tips for creating community in the classroom on the first day of school:

- Greet each student at the door as they enter.

- Organize the classroom so that it's obvious what students should do immediately and where they should sit.

- As students enter the classroom, look for ways that they interact with one another to see where they may need additional practice with communication skills in the days and weeks to come. Do they give other people a chance to talk? Do they express genuine interest in what others have to say? Do they seem comfortable speaking up with one another?

- Help students start learning their classmates' names and connecting with one another by making name tags or doing other simple activities.

- Begin to notice which students may already have strong bonds with each other. Encourage interaction with other students, as well. You can do this by mixing up seating arrangements, rotating groups, or arranging partner chats with a variety of classmates.

- Look for ways to highlight connections between students. As you discover that students have common interests, make note of them so that you can find ways to integrate those interests into lessons, Advisory topics, or casual conversations in the early days of school. Be open and honest about how students may need to stretch themselves to find commonalities. Be clear that although not everyone will be best friends in this class, everyone will work together as a community of learners.

Responsive Advisory Meeting

Although we may feel pressure to jump right into academics on the first day, taking time to focus on community-building can yield long-term benefits and better results for students' learning. Starting with the practice of Responsive Advisory Meeting (see pages 8–9) on the first day of school helps lay the foundation for a positive learning community in each classroom and in the school at large. Responsive Advisory Meeting gives students an opportunity to engage with the teacher and each other in an authentic way and start forming positive teacher-student and student-student relationships.

The goal for the first meeting is simply for students to start using each other's names, make some personal connections, and feel safe and included. At the beginning of the year, when you're just starting to build trust with students, keep your Responsive Advisory Meeting components low risk by following these guidelines:

- Keep discussions between partners (rather than larger groups)

- Choose activities that don't require any touch

- Keep sharing focused on basic information that is comfortable for students to discuss

To help ensure success, teach and model the skills students will need to complete all components. In particular, be sure to model how students should read and interact with the announcements message, and procedures for acknowledgments, such as taking turns sharing with a partner.

Here is an example of what a Responsive Advisory Meeting might look like on the first day.

Arrival Welcome

Stand at the door as you introduce yourself and ask each student their name as they enter.

Announcements

Hello, Advisory Team!

I am looking forward to all of us getting to know each other this year. Here is a self-portrait that includes an object.

What object would you include in a self-portrait (or selfie) to show something about your interests or personality? Write your response on an index card at your table.

Self-Portrait with a Harp by Rose Adélaïde Ducreux (French, Paris 1761–1802 Santo Domingo) via The Metropolitan Museum of Art is licensed under CC0 1.0.

Acknowledgments

Have students pair up with someone in their table group or nearby. In each pair, students take turns introducing themselves and sharing their response to the announcements prompt and why they chose it.

Activity

Switch: Students hold their right hand out in front of them with their thumb up and all other fingers curled in, and their left hand out in front of them with their index finger pointing forward and their thumb and other fingers curled in. When you call out "Switch!" everyone switches so that their left thumb is up and their right index finger is pointing out. Continue calling "Switch!" and having everyone switch back and forth.

 Close the meeting by asking a reflection question for students to think about as they leave Advisory: "Think ahead to the last day of this school year. How do you want that day to look and feel, both socially and academically?"

 Download a printable Responsive Advisory Meeting Planning Guide at https://www.responsiveclassroom.org/printables/.

Communication Skills

On the first day of school, there are a lot of new experiences, new people to meet, and new things to figure out. Students may feel overwhelmed by having to find their way around the building, change classes, and be apart from peers who are now on different teams or in different schools. Keep a friendly attitude and a good sense of humor, and remind students that mistakes will happen—and that's okay! Let them know that every expert in every field of study had to make mistakes in order to learn. You might even show students an example of a mistake or an early effort of an expert who later went on to success in their field. Emphasize that we learn through mistakes, and that it's okay to ask for help when needed.

Teaching communication skills and offering ideas for making connections with others can also help students feel more at ease. As they begin to form relationships with new classmates and reconnect with old friends, ideas for how to start a conversation may be helpful to them. As with other social and emotional skills, those involved in initiating a conversation need to be taught and practiced. Below are some ideas that students can use to help make connections right from the first day. You may find it helpful to display anchor charts or posters with some of these ideas in your classroom and elsewhere in school, especially at the beginning of the year.

How to Introduce Yourself

Model this process for students, and emphasize that this skill can help them both in and out of school. Have students find a partner at their table group and practice introducing themselves using the following strategies:

- Say "Hi, my name is _____. What's yours?"

- Make eye contact, and keep your facial expression friendly.

- Try memorization tricks to help you remember names. For example, think of a characteristic that begins with the same sound as the person's name: "Garrett is wearing green"; "Shonda has a shiny bracelet."

- Starting with tablemates, focus on learning a few names each day and building up over time.

Conversation Starters

You can post these or similar questions on day one as a way to get students talking. You could also use these questions during a Responsive Advisory Meeting as part of your announcements message or as topics to discuss as part of acknowledgments.

- What kind of movies do you like?

- Do you like to play video games? Which ones?

- What fun things did you do this summer?

- What would your theme song be? Why?

- What would you do on a perfect day?

- What is the farthest you have traveled from home?

- If you could live at any time in history, when would it be? Why?

Transitions and Nonclassroom Spaces

As students enter your classroom each period, you can make them feel welcome and reassured by offering a friendly greeting with good eye contact. This immediately sets the tone for a healthy and productive learning environment where everyone feels a sense of belonging. It's also important for teachers to be available in the hallways between classes to help students find their way, sort out any schedule questions, and encourage respectful behavior. Being proactive in assisting students, especially those just starting middle school, will help create a solid foundation for good behavior when students are not in the classroom.

Just as you spend time and energy setting up procedures and routines within the class-room, you need to explain and model expected behaviors for hallways, the cafeteria, and other non-classroom spaces. As always, it's important not to assume that students come to school with all the skills they need. Whether they are new to middle school or simply need a refresher after summer vacation, be sure to proactively set the standards from day one rather than waiting for misbehavior to occur. It is important for students to understand that respect and self-control are expected in every part of the campus, not just the classroom.

One crucial element of feeling a sense of belonging is knowing where you need to be and how to get there. Consider ways to orient new middle school students to the building and school grounds, such as by posting a map or recording a video tour on a mobile device and sharing it in a presentation in class. If you teach seventh or eighth grade students, consider asking for volunteers to guide newer students who are headed to the same location. (Do this discreetly so as not to put anyone on the spot, perhaps by asking for volunteers to see you at the end of class.) You can also encourage students more generally to watch throughout the day for anyone who seems like they might be lost, ask if they need help, and offer to guide them where they need to go.

Teaching Academics

It's essential for teachers to create positive energy, excitement, and high expectations for learning on the first day of school. While you may not yet have time to deliver much academic content because of all the first-day activities, inspiring students to picture themselves as capable learners and their new classrooms as safe, engaging, and welcoming will prepare them for successful academics in the weeks and months to come.

Envisioning Language

One of the ways to communicate that you see students as capable of doing the academic work ahead is through the use of positive teacher language (see pages 4–6), an essential part of setting high expectations. In particular, envisioning language can help you show students what you believe they're capable of achieving. Envisioning language is a critical tool for setting expectations in that it articulates a positive vision and conveys faith that students can achieve that vision.

You can use envisioning language to inspire students from day one, enabling them to see themselves as capable learners in the academic community that you'll build together over the school year. Envisioning language can be phrased as a statement to show students your high expectations for them, or as a question to help them develop their own positive vision of the future. For example:

- This semester, you'll discover how our local geography affects our daily lives.

- The icebreakers we're doing today will help us learn names and start getting to know each other so that we can be a strong learning community.

- By the end of this semester, you'll know how to use the pottery wheel, and you'll have made several of your own projects.

- How will working with a science partner help you learn?

- What will it look, sound, and feel like to have a successful writing workshop?

Through word choice, phrasing, tone of voice, pace, and body language, our teacher language serves as a powerful tool that influences how students think, act, and feel. On the first day of school, it's important to remember what a lasting impression our words and tone can leave. Begin the first day with words that are firm and warm, that help students recognize and build on their positive efforts and take responsibility for their work, and that convey your belief that all students want to and can be productive members of the classroom community. The expectations and beliefs you convey through your language can have a huge impact on how students view themselves and treat each other.

Academic Mindset and Academic Behaviors

For students to be successful in school, they need to develop an academic mindset and academic behaviors. An academic mindset consists of four self-perceptions:

- I belong in this academic community

- My effort improves my performance

- I can succeed at this work

- I see the value in this work

The goals for day one are designed to support an academic mindset by encouraging a community where every student feels included and by strengthening students' confidence that they are capable of doing the academic work they'll encounter this year. As previously noted, techniques such as envisioning language can help you achieve these goals and set students up for success.

Academic behaviors are specific actions students take in order to succeed in school. These include regular attendance, arriving ready to work, paying attention, participating in instructional activities and class discussions, and devoting out-of-school time to studying and completing assignments. Reinforce these behaviors as you see them to help students solidify good habits and build on their successes.

It's also important to help students develop what social psychologist Carol Dweck (2010) calls a growth mindset. As opposed to a fixed mindset, which is the belief that intelligence and abilities are unchanging characteristics, a growth mindset is the belief that one can improve their abilities and strengthen their knowledge through effort and perseverance. When you encourage this belief in students, they will be more likely to stretch their abilities, develop more effective learning strategies, and seek out learning opportunities. Explaining this mindset, reinforcing the idea that mistakes are a crucial part of the learning process, and encouraging self-reflection are all important ways to foster a growth mindset in students.

Teaching Your Content

Although much of day one will focus on helping students get oriented and begin to get to know each other, it is also the time to start introducing the content you'll be teaching over the course of the quarter, semester, or year. Use envisioning language to foster not only a sense of competence for the work ahead but also a sense of excitement: "This quarter, we're going to explore the mysteries of ancient Rome!" Share your own genuine enthusiasm about the topics you'll cover, and when you hear students mention interests that relate to your content area, point out those connections as well: "I heard you mention that you're interested in fashion design. During the unit, you'll have a chance to discover what Romans wore and how their clothes showed their social status."

On the first day of school, preview content that students will be learning by sharing a course syllabus or overview of upcoming topics. Having an understanding of what's ahead can help students feel more in control, get excited about interesting topics, and be better prepared for success. You might have each student come up with a question they'd like to investigate in an upcoming unit. They could write these questions on sticky notes and post them all on a large sheet of paper. This activity can build a sense of curiosity and strengthen the learning community by showing that no one is an expert yet, and everyone has things they'd like to discover.

You might also introduce some mnemonic devices that will assist students in remembering key concepts of the academic content to come. After providing one or more examples of existing mnemonic devices, you could have students work with a partner to create their own. Here are examples for several different subject areas:

- **Taxonomic ranks in biology**—King Philip Can Order Five Greek Salads (Kingdom, Phylum, Class, Order, Family, Genus, Species)

- **Lines on a treble staff**—Every Good Boy Does Fine (E, G, B, D, F)

- **Order of operations for equations**—Please Excuse My Dear Aunt Sally (Parentheses, Exponents, Multiplication, Division, Addition, Subtraction)

Now is also a good time to introduce the proper use of any supplies or equipment that students will need in the early days and weeks of the school year, such as musical instruments, microscopes, art supplies, computers, or athletic equipment. Use Interactive Modeling (see pages 6–7) to help students learn and practice how to use such supplies or equipment appropriately.

Interactive Learning Structures

On the first day of school, rely on interactive learning structures that are simple and low risk, allowing students to share basic information in pairs. You can combine community-building with academic content by giving students the chance to practice names and learn about each other in ways that are connected with your topic area. For example, you could use the following interactive learning structure in an English class. (Later on in the year, this activity could be done without introductions and with more in-depth class content.)

Parallel Lines

1. Name the learning goal. For example: "You're going to form two parallel lines to start meeting your classmates and talk about some of your favorite books."

2. Have students count off by twos. Ones form a line and twos form a parallel line next to it, so each two faces a one, forming a pair.

3. State a question or topic for discussion: "Introduce yourself to your partner, then tell them the name of a favorite book and why you like it." Give students some think time.

4. Partners take turns speaking for 1–2 minutes total, briefly exchanging ideas.

5. Ones stay in place while twos move up a person, with the first person in line moving to the end of the line. Everyone should now be facing a new partner. Remind students about safe movement: "How might you stay in your personal space when moving in your line?"

6. New partners introduce themselves and discuss the same question or topic, or a different one that you pose (such as their favorite literary character or book genre). Repeat as time allows. Reinforce positive behavior: "I noticed your transitions were quick and efficient. You held productive discussions with each of your partners."

Brain Breaks

On the first day of school, students may be feeling distracted or uneasy. Brain breaks (see page 10) can help them feel more calm and focused, and can also help recharge their energy in a safe and structured way. Here are a few low-risk activities that are appropriate for use on day one.

Refocusing Brain Break: Four and Eight

1. Tell students to stand and stretch, then have them sit at their desks or in a circle, closing their eyes if they wish.

2. Tell students they will take slow, deep breaths to help them focus and relax, inhaling for a count of four and exhaling for a count of eight.

3. Keep a steady beat as you count for students to hear: "*In*, two, three, four, *out*, two, three, four, five, six, seven, eight."

4. Keeping the beat without pausing, have students do several more cycles.

Recharging Brain Break: Conductor

1. Designate five or six small groups around the classroom, or use existing table clusters.

2. Assign each group a sound to make (such as a low-pitched "Hmmm" or a higher-pitched "La la la la la") and a corresponding movement to do (such as marching in place or waving their hands).

3. Stand at the front of the room as the conductor. Tell students you will use hand signals to have each group start making their sound and doing their movement (such as by pointing at them), increase or decrease their volume (such as by raising or lowering one hand), and stop making their sound and doing their movement (such as by closing your hand into a fist).

4. Start with everyone in silence, then cue one group at a time to start their sound and movement, and then increase or decrease their volume. Bring in different combinations of groups to change the overall sound of the class.

5. End by bringing in all groups, raising the volume up high, and then signaling everyone to stop together.

As you introduce new brain breaks, pay attention to which ones students like the most. Class favorites can be repeated throughout the year. As students get to know each other better, you can also vary brain breaks by having student volunteers be the leaders.

Tip: In order to keep students engaged, collaborate with your team ahead of time to plan which brain breaks each teacher will use. That way, students will experience a variety throughout the day rather than repeating the same one or two. In addition to the activities in this book, see *Refocus and Recharge! 50 Brain Breaks for Middle Schoolers* (Center for Responsive Schools, 2016) for more ideas.

Teaching Discipline

In order to create a safe classroom community in which everyone can do their best learning, it's essential to let students know what the expectations are and to demonstrate that you will enforce those expectations in a calm and respectful manner. On day one, show students that you'll be holding them to a high standard—and that you believe in their capacity to live up to that standard.

Effective Management

One of the foundations of positive behavior is good classroom management. By managing the classroom in an effective way, you can create an orderly environment that promotes autonomy and allows students to focus on learning. Classroom management strategies include organizing the space for comfort and efficiency (see pages 17–18), forming healthy teacher-student and student-student relationships, managing time, and clearly teaching specific procedures and routines. On day one, start teaching the most basic procedures students need in order to be productive and safe in your classroom, and the routines of when to do them. For example, a common procedure might be checking the board for a list of materials needed for class and taking out those materials, and the associated routine might be to complete this procedure as soon as one enters the classroom.

Modeling Good Behavior

As you prepare for the first day of school, think about the procedures you'll need to teach students and how to prioritize them. Brainstorm a list of basic tasks that students will perform, such as entering and exiting your classroom, turning in homework, or using a particular app. Teach a procedure right before students need to do it for the first time so that they will be set up for success. Model the most important procedures on the first day, but be careful not to overload students by modeling too many things at once. After making your prioritized list of procedures to teach, keep it handy to help you figure out when to teach each one over the first few weeks of school.

Also, look at your daily schedule for transitions, such as going to and returning from the cafeteria, taking bathroom breaks, or using lockers between classes. As noted on page 19, it may work well to divide up these procedures with your teammates ahead of time to ensure that modeling them is spread out over the day and that each student learns all the procedures they need.

Here's an example of how Interactive Modeling could be used on the first day to teach the proper procedure for turning in homework.

1. **Describe what you will model and why.** "Today, I'll show you the procedure for turning in homework. Watch what I do."

2. **Model while students notice.** Silently demonstrate the process of turning an assignment into the "homework" basket. After you finish, ask the students, "What did you notice about how I turned in my assignment?" Students may say, "You came into the room and set your things down on your desk first." "You got organized and found your homework before you went up to the basket." If a student puts their response in the negative, help them reframe their statement in the positive. For example, if a student says, "You didn't look at other people's assignments in the basket," respond with "What did I do?" The student might then say, "You dropped your assignment on top of the pile and went back to your desk." It might be helpful to record students' answers on a chart to refer back to as they practice during the next step.

3. **Give students the opportunity to collaborate and practice.** Say: "Now you will practice how to hand in your homework using the freewriting assignment you just did." Choose a table cluster to go first. The students get up and hand in their assignments, applying the characteristics they observed you modeling.

4. **Reinforce their practice with immediate feedback.**
Look for demonstrations of the characteristics they just named. Use reinforcing language in a general way (rather than singling students out) when you see those behaviors: "I see students taking out their assignments before they go up to the basket." "I notice people carefully placing their assignments on top of the pile." "It looks like we'll be organized and ready to learn because everyone has carefully handed in their work."

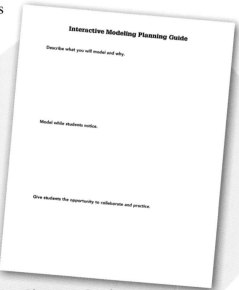

 Download a printable Interactive Modeling Planning Guide at https://www.responsiveclassroom.org/printables/.

Reinforcing Language

As you see students successfully completing the procedures you've taught, being kind and helpful to one another, and following classroom rules on day one, you can use reinforcing language (see page 5) to encourage and build on their efforts. Recognizing students' positive actions with honest, specific feedback helps them understand what they're doing well and stay motivated to continue those actions. Reinforcing language can be addressed to the whole group or (privately) to an individual, and you might choose to use open-ended follow-up questions to help students consider how to build on their actions. Here are some examples:

- I noticed people double-checking their work before turning it in.

- Everyone is patiently waiting for their turn to talk. What's helping you do that?

- Jacqui, you were so helpful in the hallway just now. I saw you show several new students how to find their way to class.

- Marc, I saw you working hard on your self-portrait. Your effort really shows in all the details you've included. What helped you stay focused?

Throughout the first day—both in and outside your classroom—use reinforcing language when students make choices or exhibit behaviors that you want to encourage and see throughout the year.

Introducing the Rules

Teaching students about the rules is an ongoing process throughout the year. That process includes discussion, practice, and reinforcement of the rules, with a focus on how the rules can help everyone meet their goals and be successful in and out of school. The process starts on day one by introducing the rules.

Middle school students have attended school for years, but they still need to learn your particular classroom's rules and become invested in them. Even if you have a common set of rules for the whole school that students in the older grades are already familiar with, it's important to take time on the first day to go over those rules again. After a summer away from school, it's good to have a refresher of what the expectations are. Plus, as students mature, they often develop a new appreciation for what the rules mean.

The rules need to be clear from the start so that you're able to reinforce good behavior and redirect misbehavior—and so that students know what is expected of them. Introducing a rule only after it's broken can erode trust between a teacher and a student, so it's critical for the sake of your relationships with students to be transparent from the start.

As you go over the rules on day one, let students know that the rules are guidelines designed to help them meet their goals, and that you'll be talking about these rules on an ongoing basis throughout the year. Consider posting a list of the rules in your classroom or another visible space so that students can easily see them and refer to them as needed.

Responding to Misbehavior

It's to be expected that students will make mistakes and test limits on the first day of school. When students misbehave, they—and everyone in the class—need to see that you will be a strong and respectful leader and will respond to all students in a calm yet firm manner. In week two, you will begin teaching logical consequences, which offer different options for responding to misbehavior. For the first day and the rest of this week, keep things simple by using reminding and redirecting language and basic visual cues, which are self-explanatory to students and can be used immediately.

After you've introduced the rules, students need to know that you will enforce those rules in a consistent and respectful way. If one or more students are beginning to get off task, use reminding language (see page 5) to help them meet the expectations they've learned so far. You might discreetly ask a student who's doodling instead of doing a writing exercise, "Shana, look back over the writing prompt. What's the first step of the assignment?" If the class as a whole is getting too loud during a partner chat activity, you might say to everyone, "Show me how you can control your volume so that people can hear each other."

If off-task behavior escalates or continues, or if a misbehavior is serious enough to be disruptive, use redirecting language (see page 5) to give students clear, nonnegotiable directions about what they should be doing. Unlike reminding language, which assumes students are able to make good decisions in the moment, redirecting language lets the teacher take over when a student is not showing self-control in the moment. Delivered in a calm tone at the first sign of misbehavior, redirecting language lets students know you're serious about the rules and helps them improve their behavior while preserving their dignity.

Here are some examples of off-task behaviors needing immediate redirection that you might see on the first day of school, with examples of redirecting language you might use to address them. Unless a redirection is being given to the entire class, try to deliver redirecting language to the student quietly and discreetly in order to avoid embarrassment.

Using Redirecting Language

Scenario	What You Might Say
Samuel bangs his locker closed and walks away, running his hand across all the lockers and banging the locks as he goes.	"Samuel, stop. Go back to your locker and try again."
Madison is eager to talk with friends who are on a different team. As she makes her way down the hall, she ignores a handful of papers that fall out of her book bag.	"Madison, go back and pick up your papers."
Anaya points out another girl's outfit and makes a rude comment.	"Anaya, polite and respectful comments only."
Ginger snatches a pencil out of another student's hand during group work.	"Ginger, give the pencil back and go get one from the supply shelf."
Jake skips past people in the lunch line, saying that they're moving too slowly.	"Jake, go back to your spot in line and wait your turn."
Several students notice the clock and decide that it's time to change classes. The whole class starts packing up to go.	"Everyone, take your seats. Wait until I give the signal for ending class."
Lee gets up during a table-group discussion and sits down next to a friend at a different table.	"Lee, go back to your group."
Julio keeps working on his writing project after writing time ends and a whole-class discussion begins.	"Julio, stop. It's time to move on."

Sometimes, the simplest and most effective way to stop an unwanted behavior doesn't involve any words at all. A visual cue—like making eye contact or nodding at a student—lets them know that you see what they're doing, and that you both know they need to change their behavior. Another effective cue is to walk over and stand near a student or group of students who are starting to get off task. These types of cues can be done without any interruption to instruction and will often be enough to get students to do what they're supposed to do without any further effort from you. (Of course, if a student does not change their behavior after receiving one of these cues, you can follow up with redirecting language, or later, with a logical consequence.)

These sorts of signals let students know that you believe in their ability to regain self-control and follow the rules, and can thus help you in establishing positive teacher-student relationships. Use visual cues and teacher proximity as soon as possible when you notice behavior beginning to go awry, before it escalates. Be sure to keep your body language calm and neutral. If you are visibly angry or frustrated, simple eye contact can carry a much more judgmental message. Finally, don't overuse visual cues—if students know you will give them multiple cues before escalating to redirection, they are less likely to take your cues seriously.

Getting Ready for Goal-Setting

When students are invested in the rules, they are more likely to be intrinsically motivated to contribute to a safe, focused, and enjoyable classroom environment, and the way they become invested is by seeing how the rules can help them achieve their personal goals. Thus, the first step toward getting students invested in the rules is goal-setting.

On the first day of school, students are just getting acclimated to new classes and routines, so it's too early for them to put serious thought into setting goals for the quarter, semester, or year. However, you can plant some seeds to get students thinking about what their goals might be. Asking open-ended questions as part of Responsive Advisory Meeting or as students review the syllabus can be a way to prime their thinking for when it's time to work on setting SMART goals later in the week. These questions might include the following:

- What are some topics in the syllabus you are interested in learning more about?

- Think about a success you had last year in school. What do you think helped lead to that success?

- What is a skill or type of support that you might need in order to be successful in this class?

- Our work in this class will help you become better thinkers this year. How do you think the course content will stretch your thinking this year?

Students can be asked to reflect on these questions silently or do a quick freewriting exercise. You could ask students to turn in their ideas to you. Because it is the first day, asking students to share with one another may be too high-risk.

Reference
Dweck, Carol. 2010. *Mindset: The New Psychology of Success.* New York: Ballantine Books.

The Rest of Week One

And let us not forget that even one book, one pen,
one child, and one teacher can change the world.

—Malala Yousafzai, human rights activist and the youngest
winner of the Nobel Peace Prize at age 17

The remainder of the first week of school follows through on the foundational work started on day one. While it may feel challenging to think about fitting community- and relationship-building into a busy academic schedule, remember that social-emotional and academic success support each other. Because significant cognitive growth occurs through social interaction, the time you put in now to strengthen students' connections both with you and with each other can help you build a stronger learning community in which students can succeed throughout the entire year.

The ultimate goal is to build a cooperative and collaborative classroom, where students can develop academic, social, and emotional competencies and master rigorous academic content and skills. Creating a learning space that reflects and responds to each student's needs will pay off in greater academic success throughout the rest of the year.

Goals for Week One

The goals for the rest of week one focus on creating conditions for every student to be academically, socially, and behaviorally successful. One of the guiding principles of the *Responsive Classroom* approach states that what we know and believe about students individually, culturally, and developmentally informs our expectations of, reactions to, and attitudes about those students. Use this time to get to know students so that all your interactions with them can be intentional, informed, and positive.

1. **Foster positive teacher-student and student-student connections.** This week is a prime time for students to continue getting to know you and each other through low-risk community-building interactions. Teach content using simple interactive learning structures to help build a community where trust and cooperation thrive.

2. **Create a classroom that is safe, predictable, and conducive to learning.** Effective classroom management and well-designed lessons are essential for reducing misbehavior, keeping students engaged and on task, and setting students up for academic and behavioral success.

3. **Assess students' academic skills, and offer opportunities to practice.** Take time to observe students to determine whether they have satisfactory prior knowledge for the concepts you'll be teaching. Think about individual learning styles, and provide opportunities for practicing essential skills for success.

4. **Teach students how to set SMART goals.** Guide students in setting academic, social, and behavioral goals for school that are SMART: specific, measurable, achievable, relevant, and time-bound. In addition to helping students make progress in areas that matter to them, this process is the first step in investing students in the rules.

Creating Conditions for Success

As you continue through week one, making connections is a priority so that students' sense of belonging and significance may continue growing. Our brains are wired to build social connections, and the young adolescent brain craves being engaged in the social world and interacting with others.

Building Community

As you proceed through the first week of school, remember to be a role model for respect and set expectations for respect as a cornerstone of all interactions. Within the classroom, respect begins when teachers help students feel visible and significant, hold high standards, and set positive expectations for behavior and achievement. In the first two or three days, learn and use students' names; pay attention to keeping your tone and body language positive; and be approachable, empathetic, and firm.

To continue helping students connect with one another, you might try giving table groups a minute or two to chat about a social question you pose at the beginning of class or before launching a more structured activity: "Before we start today's lesson, take a couple of minutes to share with your tablemates where you would go if you could travel to any other country in the world, and one reason why you want to go there." Also, remind students to make a point to continue learning each other's names. If you're using name tags or cards, remind students to refer to those and address one another by name to practice. For times when students are in the hallway or other areas where they might not have name tags or cards with them, discuss and model how to politely ask someone's name, especially if you've forgotten it.

Responsive Advisory Meeting

Advisory will vary from one middle school to the next, so you may have an Advisory period every day or only on certain days of the week. Either way, now is the time to settle into the routine of Advisory and give students the opportunity to practice the four components of the Responsive Advisory Meeting structure. By understanding and feeling comfortable with this structure, students can participate more fully because they know what to expect.

Continue using straightforward, low-risk meetings throughout this week. Use Interactive Modeling to demonstrate the skills students will need for success, and reminding language to keep them on task. Some skills you might model this week include greeting others respectfully, entering the classroom and reading the announcements message, and making appropriate eye contact while speaking.

One of the goals during week one is to help students start making positive connections with other students and with you. For the first week, keep acknowledgments very basic and low-risk. Teach and model essential social skills, such as how to welcome others into a group. Having the ability to welcome others is especially important this early in the school year, when schedule changes may still be occurring, new students may still be enrolling, and some students may feel isolated from others.

To keep Responsive Advisory Meeting low-risk in the first week of school, consider the following advice for each component:

- **Arrival Welcome**—Keep physical contact minimal or nonexistent, depending on what feels right for your classroom. Consider offering a wave or other variations as you greet students.

- **Announcements**—Have students do a silent reflection or a reflection that is only seen by the teacher if the topic goes beyond basic information or interests.

- **Acknowledgments**—Keep groups small. Students greet one or more tablemates and engage in a conversation prompt.

- **Activity**—Elicit a shared response from the table to foster students' connections with one another.

Here are a few examples of what the components may look like this week.

Arrival Welcome

Stand at the door and welcome students by name as they enter. Consider offering a friendly gesture (without physical contact), like a nod or a wave.

Announcements

Welcome Back, Scholars!

Think about what you need in order to succeed academically. What is one thing your teachers could do to support your learning this year? Write your name and response on an index card at your table.

Upcoming events: Extracurricular Activities Fair this Friday at lunch, outside the cafeteria

Acknowledgments

What's the News?: In each table group, one student begins by greeting the student to their left and asking what the news is: "Good morning, Sonia. What's the news?" The student greeted returns the greeting, shares something that's going on in their life, and then turns and greets the next person: "Good morning, Tim. The news is my grandmother is visiting this weekend. Good morning, Jaya. What's the news?" This continues around the table until all students have been greeted and have shared their news.

Activity

Snowball: Hand out a piece of paper to each student and tell them not to write their names on their papers. Ask students to write down one person they admire and why. Write down your response, too. Then, have everyone crumple up their piece of paper into a "snowball" and toss it into the middle of the room. Everyone picks up a nearby snowball and takes turns reading their snowball aloud.

 Close the meeting by having students look at their response to the announcements prompt. Have them hand their cards in to you and then reflect on the following question: "What are some ways you can seek help when you feel stuck or aren't sure what to do next?"

 Download a printable Responsive Advisory Meeting Planning Guide at https://www.responsiveclassroom.org/printables/.

Transitions and Nonclassroom Spaces

Using reinforcing language effectively can make a positive difference during tricky times, like transitions. Think about some transitions or areas where problems may occur. Note the following examples of reinforcing language you could use when you see positive behaviors at these times or in these areas:

- In the hallway: "I see everyone walking at a safe and reasonable pace to get to class on time."

- Turning in class materials and supplies: "Everyone was patient and waited for others to finish before putting supplies back where they came from."

- Getting to class on time: "You all got to class on time. That lets us get to work right away."

- In the cafeteria: "When you get everything that you need while in the lunch line, it gives you more time to enjoy your lunch."

- During assemblies: "You are getting in line respectfully."

- During arrival time: "You all helped keep the hallways safe by making sure the entrance was clear."

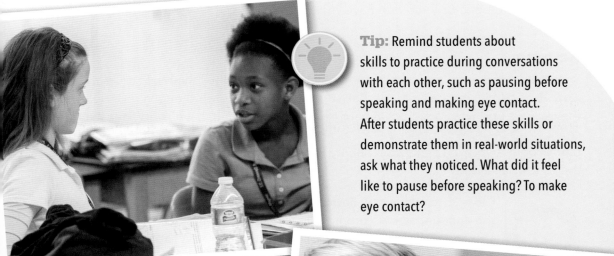

Tip: Remind students about skills to practice during conversations with each other, such as pausing before speaking and making eye contact. After students practice these skills or demonstrate them in real-world situations, ask what they noticed. What did it feel like to pause before speaking? To make eye contact?

Closing the School Day

The practice of closing the day gives students time to reflect on academic content and the overall school day, to mentally prepare for upcoming school events, or to simply recharge their energy to get ready to come back the next school day. This practice takes place at the end of the last period of the day and allows the whole class to come together for 5–10 minutes in a brief conversation or simple activity.

As you observe students, think about what they need. They might need time to recharge at the end of an intense day, to reflect quietly through writing or drawing, or to reconnect with classmates in an interactive activity. During this first week and throughout the school year, closing the day will help students practice self-regulation and prepare to come back to school refreshed the next day.

A brief discussion focused on a particular topic or question is a helpful and simple way to close the day during the first week. Here are some sample reflection questions you might choose from this week:

Sixth Graders

- What went well for you today?
- What could be an improvement for tomorrow?
- How did you meet new people today?
- What is one thing you are looking forward to this school year?

Seventh Graders

- How is the first day of seventh grade different from the first day of sixth grade?
- What was a positive moment you had today?
- What is a hope you have for this first week of school?
- Did you meet new classmates today? How did you "break the ice" with them?

Eighth Graders

- What was a positive moment you had today? What actions led to that moment?
- What is a hope you have for this first quarter of the school year?
- What's one thing you can do this week to start the year off on the right foot?
- How might you help a friend who is struggling to get focused this week?

Working With Your Team

Later in this chapter, you'll learn about setting SMART goals with students this week. Because students may have different SMART goals for each of their classes, they'll need help keeping their various goals organized. You'll also need a way to record the SMART goals of the students in all your classes and monitor their progress toward reaching those goals.

Work with your team to create a unified system for helping students store and organize their SMART goals. For example, you might decide that each teacher will instruct all students to store their SMART goal planner for each class at the beginning of the relevant section in their binder. Or, teachers can create a poster for each class on which students can write down their SMART goal and sign their name, allowing the collective goals for that class to be posted so everyone can see them and support each other's progress.

Think about what system will best help you organize and track students' progress toward their SMART goals. You might keep a written list of students' goals in a binder of your own, with room for notes, or you could record SMART goals electronically in a spreadsheet. An effective system will allow you to refer to students' goals frequently and make notes on a regular basis.

Teaching Academics

As academics begin in earnest this week, continue providing opportunities for students to get to know each other and build the classroom community. Now is also the time to start assessing students' content knowledge as well as their basic academic skills, and to provide support and practice where needed.

Having students work cooperatively in teams toward the same objective is a classroom strategy that provides all students opportunities to think, engage in academic talk, and reflect individually and together. This strategy thus helps students develop cooperation skills, responsibility, and teamwork while emphasizing the ideas of fairness and inclusion.

Throughout this week, continue teaching and modeling the academic routines and foundational skills students will need in order to be successful throughout the year. Also, be mindful of how much information students are taking in during the first week. In addition to academics, they're learning new routines, following new schedules, finding new classrooms, and meeting new classmates and teachers. Be ready with lesson plans that will engage them and plenty of brain breaks to help them recharge and absorb all the new things they're learning.

Modeling Academic Skills

As you take time this week to assess students' academic skills, think about the basic academic procedures they'll need to know in order to be successful this year, such as:

- How to ask for help if they're stuck

- Methods for keeping track of assignments

- Ways to keep track of time during an activity

- What to do if they finish a task and have time left over

- Note-taking and highlighting techniques

Establishing a few essential academic procedures at the beginning of the school year will help students start to move toward greater autonomy with their academic work and become more self-motivated as learners. It will also empower teachers to be successful with active teaching (see page 11). Students' ability to function independently is what allows us to provide individual coaching, meet separately with small groups, and deliver academic lessons that engage all students. You can teach these routines using Interactive Modeling, and then redirect, remind, and reinforce students as they work toward mastering them.

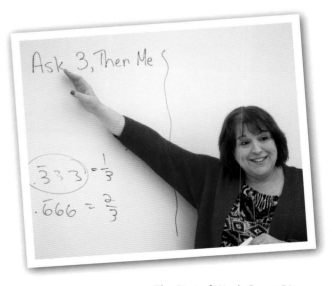

To set students up for success with homework, introduce it this week. Homework should be assigned with a clear objective in mind—to practice a skill, prepare for an assessment, extend learning, or integrate a skill with other learning. A consistent homework schedule can help students remember to do assignments—every Monday and Thursday night, for example. Take time with students this week to discuss:

- How much homework will be assigned

- When homework will be assigned, and when it will be due

- When, where, and how to turn homework in

- How to find assignments they've missed while absent

- Why homework is important, and the potential consequences to their grades and classroom experience if assignments are not completed

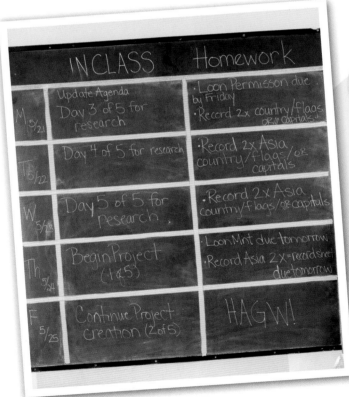

Tip: Put homework expectations in writing and display them for reference to help increase the chances of assignments being completed successfully.

Speaking and Listening Skills

One of the most notable developmental changes in middle school students is their increasing ability to organize their thinking and express it verbally. Support the continued growth of this cognitive ability by using strategies and structures that give all students the responsibility and opportunity for verbal participation, connecting lessons to real-world events or examples, and allowing students to practice their new skills in small group discussions or partner chats.

Teachers also need to make sure they're not the ones doing most of the talking in the classroom. Cognitive growth and academic achievement depend on students' spending time talking about what they are learning. When asking questions to give students opportunities to talk, it's important to rely primarily on questions that allow for discussion rather than those that simply check for understanding. In responding to the latter sort of question, some students may try to figure out what the teacher wants them to say, while those who are waiting for the answer may check out.

Using interactive learning structures and giving students clear and explicit directions for how to complete the task of co-constructing knowledge as they talk create a sense of shared responsibility and ownership for their learning. These opportunities for academic talk also allow for the sharing of different personal and cultural perspectives. For example, after reading a passage that depicts the life of a young adolescent, invite students to discuss how it is similar to or different from their own experiences. As students share, reinforce the importance of listening to and having empathy for one another's stories.

This week, take time to model good communication skills as a way to support students in having productive academic discussions. After using Interactive Modeling to teach essential communication skills, consider posting a chart like the one that follows to offer reminders about and additional practice in communicating respectfully. You can have students practice these skills both with academic content and in ways that are directly focused on building student relationships.

Communication Skills

Skill	Characteristics	How to Practice
Speaking Confidently	• Maintaining a relaxed but straight posture • Making eye contact • Speaking at an appropriate volume and pace	• Turn and talk with a partner • Share a simple piece of personal or academic information
Expressing Opinions	• Using supporting details • Sequencing ideas logically • Understanding the difference between fact and opinion	• Use sentence starters during a partner chat, such as "I think…" "I believe…" "In my opinion…" • Refer to prompting questions: "Is that your opinion or a fact?"
Asking Questions	• Being genuinely curious about what the other person has to say • Maintaining a respectful tone and body language	• Brainstorm questions after watching a video clip • Reflect on the types of questions they have asked
Listening	• Smiling or nodding appropriately • Thinking about what the speaker is saying	• Focus on respectful listening during partner chats • Share what their partner said after a discussion

Teaching Your Content

This week, let students know about regular features and occurrences to expect in your classroom. For example:

- A math teacher who posts a "Problem of the Day" each day could note that the problem will connect to that day's content or skills and could describe where to find the problem, where to look for help solving it, and what to do once they've completed it.

- A language arts teacher who has students read a passage and respond to a reflection question each week could hand out notebooks or explain how to record responses digitally; discuss the type of responses they're looking for in terms of length, content, and structure; and ask students what types of books they like and would be interested in writing about.

- A science teacher could hand out lab notebooks that will be used for collecting data when doing scientific laboratory work and could introduce the requirements for keeping the notebook through the use of a small low-risk investigation. The first week is also a good time to prepare for upcoming experiments by having students sign a lab safety contract.

Interactive Learning Structures

Over the course of this week, continue fostering positive teacher-student and student-student connections by using interactive learning structures that allow students to share details about themselves.

Four Corners

1. Pose a question that has four possible responses, and designate one corner of the room for each response. Examples: "Where would you like to go on vacation? The beach, an amusement park, another country, staycation." "What genre of book do you like best? Sci-fi, mystery, biography, realistic fiction." "If you were on a deserted island, which item would you like to have? Book, iPod with favorite music, fishing pole, treasure map."

2. Give students a minute to reflect on their choice. When time is up, have them move to the corresponding corner. Reinforce positive behavior: "I noticed you carefully considered your choice before moving to that corner."

3. In their corners, students partner up, greet each other by name, and discuss why they made their choice, with reasons and evidence to support their decision.

4. Allow about 30 seconds for each person to share or 1–2 minutes total for a more free-flowing discussion. Provide a 10-second warning before time is up.

5. Repeat with new questions as time allows.

This structure can also be used to start incorporating academic content. For example, in a social studies class where students will be learning about different cultures, you might ask questions like, "Which country are you most interested in learning about? China, India, Ghana, Brazil." They can then discuss with their partner what interests them about their choice and what they would like to investigate about that country. This not only helps students connect with one another but also primes them for learning and gets them excited about the content to come.

Brain Breaks

Short brain breaks that are easy to teach, quick to do, and good for transitioning students from one activity to another are perfect for use during the first week of school. Here are some brain breaks to try this week.

Refocusing Brain Break: Picture This

1. Have students stand by their desks and do a few simple movements, such as stretching their arms overhead and shaking out their legs, then have them sit back down.

2. Tell students to take a deep breath and close their eyes. Then slowly guide them through the following visualization: "Think about something you really like doing. It could be walking your dog, hanging out with a friend—anything that makes you happy . . . Imagine yourself doing this activity . . . What do you see? . . . What do you hear? . . . What do you feel?"

3. Close the activity by saying, "Now imagine that it's time to end the activity . . . As you finish, you feel peaceful, relaxed . . ." Give students a few moments to end their visualizations, then say, "On three, open your eyes. One, two, three."

4. Ask volunteers to share what they visualized, as time allows.

Recharging Brain Break: The Wave

1. Students stand around the room in a rough circle, with enough space between them to enable them to safely make the motions.

2. The leader models a movement, such as raising and then lowering their arms or clapping their hands gently together. One at a time, students repeat the movement so that it travels around the circle.

3. Once the movement returns to the person who started it, the next person begins a new movement, which proceeds around the circle in the same way as the first movement.

4. Continue in this way, with as many students having a turn to initiate a movement as time allows.

Teaching Discipline

This week, keep an eye out for any behaviors—like teasing or excluding others—that might negatively affect the classroom community you're working to create. Reinforce acts of kindness when you see them, and quickly redirect any unkind behavior. Make your expectations for positive interactions clear, and stand behind them calmly and firmly. This will help you encourage healthy connections between students and a productive learning environment, which are essential as you begin the process of investing students in the rules.

Working With the Rules

Once students have been introduced to the classroom or school rules on the first day and have learned the basic routines, the process of investing students in the rules can begin. This process has four steps:

1. Setting SMART goals

2. Connecting goals to the rules

3. Connecting rules to concrete behavior

4. Making the rules come alive

This week, the focus is on step one. The process of setting SMART goals lets students know that their goals are valued and encourages them to take responsibility for their own learning.

Step 1: Setting SMART Goals

As the first week progresses, have students articulate one or more SMART goals for the year. SMART goals are:

Specific—The goal is well defined and focused, and the student understands the benefits of setting it.

Measurable—There is a clear endpoint or amount of progress the student is aiming for.

Achievable—It is realistic for the student to complete the goal with a reasonable amount of effort.

Relevant—The goal will make a positive difference in the student's life and will help them improve their own specific situation.

Time-bound—There is a deadline for achieving the goal.

SMART goals can be behavioral, academic, or social. The student is responsible for deciding—they must simply choose goals that they are able to work on in school. As an introduction to the process, consider sharing your own goal to demonstrate that learning and growth are lifelong processes and to show students that this classroom is a safe and respectful place to share what truly matters to them.

Waiting until later in the week to set SMART goals is advisable, as this will allow some time for students to start building trust with you and with each other. Young adolescents can be self-conscious and may defensively set superficial goals or make a joke out of goal-setting if they fear the judgment of their peers. If the class as a whole isn't taking goal-setting seriously, they may need a little more time before they feel safe opening up about what really matters to them. In that time, pay close attention to your interactions with students and their interactions with each other, being sure to quickly redirect any disrespectful situations. For individual students who are having a hard time opening up to goal-setting, try a one-on-one conversation combining a light touch with serious intent.

To begin the goal-setting process, have students think about possible behavioral, academic, or social goals for the year ahead or for a shorter time period, such as the first month or quarter. The following questions can help students reflect on what they want and form SMART goals. Consider asking students these questions or posting them for reference as students brainstorm.

Behavioral Goals

These goals focus on the behaviors that support students' success in school.

Sample prompts for helping students write a SMART behavioral goal:

- What might help you develop greater self-control?
- What skills might help you stay focused and on task during class?

Examples of SMART behavioral goals:

- This quarter, practice being assertive by taking on a leadership role in art club.
- By the end of this month, learn three new strategies for managing feelings of anxiety.

Academic Goals

When considering academic goals, young adolescents will benefit from coaching and from being asked genuine questions about how they'd like to develop or improve their unique abilities. Refer students to the syllabus or course overview to remind them what they'll be working on and to get them thinking about what they'll need in order to achieve success.

Sample prompts for helping students write a SMART academic goal:

- What would you like to achieve academically this year?
- How can you demonstrate learning in a particular unit?

Examples of SMART academic goals:

- Earn a B+ or better in math this quarter.
- By the end of this semester, learn two new revision skills for writing papers.

Social Goals

As young adolescents explore their emerging identities, they often define themselves as part of a peer group. Thus, they need support and guidance in identifying peers who will support them in positive ways and in exploring how they can be a good friend to others.

Sample prompts for helping students write a SMART social goal:

- What do you think are some of the qualities of a healthy friendship?
- What are some ways to make positive connections with other people in school?

Examples of SMART social goals:

- This semester, approach two new people to talk to each month.
- Practice conversation skills with a friend each week this quarter.

Have students fill in a SMART goal planner to list what their goal for your class is, what steps they need to take to achieve their goal, what milestones they'll look for to see progress, and their target date for achieving the goal. You might choose to collect students' SMART goal planners at the end of class so that you can record their goals and offer any feedback or clarifying questions that might help them refine their goals. You can return the planners the next day with instructions for how to keep their goals for all classes organized (see page 50 for more information).

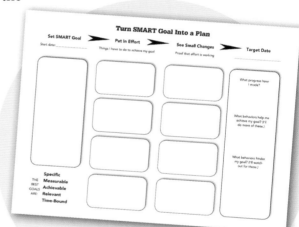

 Download a printable SMART goal planner template at https://www.responsiveclassroom.org/printables/.

Week Two

Intelligence plus character—that is the goal of true education.

—Martin Luther King Jr., civil rights leader

By week two, the school day starts to take on a more comfortable feel as procedures become routine, students start to settle into behavioral and academic habits, and positive community and a climate of lively learning begin to blossom. Therefore, week two is a great time to focus on preventing off-task behaviors and misbehaviors and encouraging the development of responsible behavior and self-control. Establishing clear expectations is a proactive strategy for setting students—and yourself—up for success, as you can refer to these expectations when the inevitable challenges, snags, and hurdles come up during the school year.

Goals for Week Two

Looking at week two through the lens of establishing expectations, the goals center on promoting habits and behaviors that support high-quality learning and prevent or reduce common misbehaviors. In week two, the focus is on promptly stopping misbehavior and helping students develop and demonstrate skills that support responsibility, assertiveness, and academic behaviors.

1. **Establish expectations for self-control.** It's important for students to learn that the classroom norm is for them to be in control of themselves. This includes being responsible for remembering expectations on their own, recognizing and managing their emotions, and controlling their behavior so that they can be successful in the moment and remain on a positive trajectory.

2. **Establish expectations for academic behaviors.** Students come to your classroom with varying levels of skill in the key academic behaviors they need in order to be successful, such as coming to class on time, completing homework, and participating productively in academic conversations. Helping them reinforce these skills will serve them well in middle school and set them up for success in high school and beyond.

3. **Invest students in the rules.** This process starts with the SMART goals students set in week one and goes on to show how classroom rules are designed to support all students in achieving those goals. In becoming invested in the rules, students continue to build connections with their classmates, develop a sense of belonging in and responsibility for a positive learning community, and start to realize how their behaviors contribute to their own success and affect others.

4. **Teach logical consequences.** Making mistakes is part of learning—and that applies to mistakes with behavior, too. Using logical consequences (as opposed to punishment) can help students develop self-control and a desire to follow the rules. Logical consequences maintain the dignity of the student and allow learning to proceed for everyone in the classroom community.

Creating Conditions for Success

Week two is a period of establishing expectations for positive behavior and academic achievement. This week, focus on naming and describing what is expected of students as members of the classroom community, how to meet those expectations, and how you will help them successfully meet those expectations.

Building Community

Although the focus this week is largely on rules and expectations, the work of establishing connections should continue. By this point, you will hopefully be seeing students using each other's names and starting to gel as a cohesive classroom and school community. Keep providing a variety of opportunities for students to interact as a way of encouraging these connections.

Responsive Advisory Meeting

The second week of school is a good time to focus Responsive Advisory Meeting on the purpose of supporting academic readiness. Take the opportunity to have students reflect on what they need to do to achieve the SMART goals they set last week, and to keep students thinking about those goals. This is also an ideal time to begin to build advisor-advisee relationships, with a focus on helping foster independence by developing skills related to responsibility and assertiveness. Here are a few ideas that you might include in Responsive Advisory Meeting this week.

Arrival Welcome

Stand at the door and welcome students by name as they enter. While some students may be pleased to be greeted by name, others will take a little warming up. To help them settle into the routine of being welcomed and returning the greeting, you might create a particular handshake or greeting that is just for your Advisory and use it all week long. This gives students a reassuring sense of predictability and can help build a group identity for your Advisory.

Announcements

Good Morning, Goal-Setters!

Think about the SMART goals you set last week. What is one obstacle you might need to overcome to meet your goals? Write your response on a sticky note at your table.

Reminder: All-school assembly today, sixth period

Acknowledgments

Have students greet their tablemates and then take turns sharing their responses to the announcements prompt.

Activity

Give each table group a piece of chart paper. Have each group brainstorm ways to overcome the obstacles they identified in response to the announcements prompt and then write their ideas on the paper. Reserve a few minutes at the end for students to walk around the room and see what ideas other groups generated.

 To close the meeting, ask students a reflection question: "How could you help a friend who is trying to reach a particular goal?"

 Download a printable Responsive Advisory Meeting Planning Guide at https://www.responsiveclassroom.org/printables/.

Closing the School Day

If you haven't already done so, introduce the circle gathering as an option for closing the day in week two. The structure of the circle can help build a sense of community by allowing all students to participate and feel seen and heard. Also, in a circle, everyone can make eye contact with everyone else, which facilitates conversation.

Use Interactive Modeling to teach students the necessary skills and procedures for gathering in a circle. These may include:

- How to efficiently clear the space for the circle

- Where to stand or sit to form the circle (including using an area outside the classroom if there is not enough space in the classroom)

- How to come to the circle prepared (calmly, respectful of others' space and movement, empty-handed)

- How to behave in ways that build trust in the circle

- How to listen and share in the circle

In closing each day this week, focus on the academic and personal expectations you want students to meet. You could use one of the following prompts for discussion:

- What was especially satisfying to you about the work you did today? Consider either the process or the outcome.

- What did you learn about a topic today that you didn't know before?

- What is one way your work met the expectations or standards that were set for it?

- What did you learn about yourself as you interacted with others?

- What's one thing you did today that you would do differently if you had a chance, and why?

- What are you excited about for tomorrow?

- In what way might you prepare so you can do your best tomorrow?

In addition to a structured discussion, feel free to use interactive learning structures, brain breaks, or silent reflections to engage students in closing the day. As you observe students and get to know them, it will become clearer which activities and reflections will best meet their needs for closing the day.

Working With Your Team

Continue taking time to coordinate with your colleagues on building a strong team. Working together, think about ways to encourage a sense of team identity while also varying activities enough so that students remain engaged. Consider the following ideas:

- Discuss Responsive Advisory Meeting activities you plan to do this week that will support the goals of week two. This early in the school year, it might be worthwhile for all Advisory groups on the team to do the same or similar activities so that students across the team will have common ground through which they can connect with one another.

- Start a shared bank of brain breaks and interactive learning structures that seem to work well with your group of students. Explore what's working and why, and discuss any areas where students may need more support so that it can be provided throughout the team. You and your colleagues can try out new ideas from the bank so that students will experience a satisfying variety of activities.

- Discuss how you will introduce and implement logical consequences on the team. Check in regularly about any discipline issues, and stay in communication about persistent challenges.

- Coordinate a team gathering where students can assist in creating a team crest or mascot to foster a stronger sense of group identity.

Teaching Academics

During the second week, continue the foundational work that was started in week one: helping students master academic routines, introducing content and materials, teaching essential small group and core speaking and listening skills, and creating an engaging and developmentally responsive learning experience. This work supports the week two goal to establish expectations for academic behaviors.

By week two, students should be starting to correctly perform classroom procedures on their own. However, there will still be areas where they need support. Keep reinforcing progress and guiding them toward positive classroom behaviors, all the while thinking about ways you can help them build confidence and feel empowered to help themselves.

Teaching Your Content

By week two, you have probably handed out textbooks. Giving students the opportunity to become familiar with their textbooks can help them prepare and get energized for the material ahead. One strategy for helping students get to know their textbook is to have a textbook scavenger hunt. This activity can also be adapted to maps, charts, classroom reference books, and other materials.

Here's an example of a filled-in scavenger-hunt sheet used for exploring a geography textbook.

Textbook Scavenger Hunt

Your name: _Ari_

Textbook title: _World Geography_

Directions: Work with your teammates to find the following information.

Table of Contents
- Find the first page of the Table of Contents and write the page number: _xii_
- What are three sections that especially interest you? _cities, rain forests, Australia_

Index
- Page number: _131_
- A topic that has multiple pages of information listed: _deserts_

Chapters
- Find the first page of a chapter. Write the chapter title and page number: _Latitude and Longitude, page 78_
- Find the last page of that same chapter. Write the page number: _89_

Images
- Find a photograph that you find interesting. Write the page number: _93_
- Study the photograph and its caption. What is one thing you learned? _Arctic and alpine are the two types of tundra_
- Locate a chart, a map, or another type of graphic in your textbook. Write the page number: _108_
- How does this image help you learn new concepts? _This map helps me learn about causes of soil salinization and where they happen in Europe_

Key Terms
- List three boldface key terms you found within one chapter: _savanna, steppe, veld_
- List two ways you can use a textbook to find the meanings of words: _look for definitions after bold or italic words, use the glossary_

 Download a printable Textbook Scavenger Hunt template at https://www.responsiveclassroom.org/printables/.

Anchoring Supports

Another strategy to consider this week is the use of anchoring supports. Just as an anchor keeps a boat in place, charts and other visual displays keep students on task by reinforcing academic content and classroom procedures and expectations. Effective anchoring supports are concise, focused, and easy to reference, and are removed when they are no longer needed.

Anchoring supports have numerous benefits:

- They reinforce academic and social-emotional skills as well as expectations essential for positive and respectful behavior, community-building, and productive learning.

- They offer a simple way to remind students of academic, behavioral, and social expectations in classroom and nonclassroom spaces.

- They empower students to remind themselves of essential content or steps before starting a task, as they work, and when they get stuck.

- They enable teachers to teach more rigorously by allowing students who need more practice or support to find that support in a self-directed way.

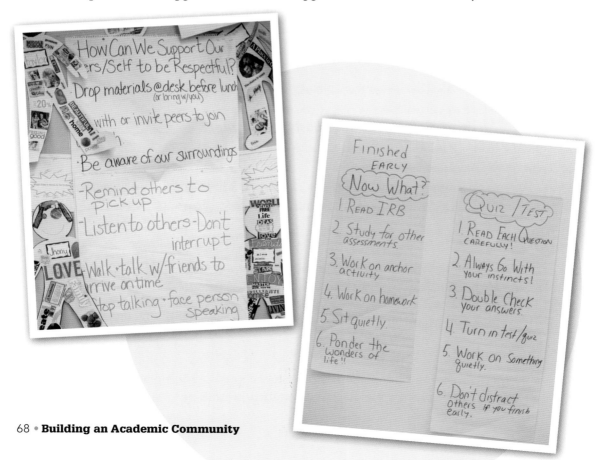

One type of support that can be helpful is the anchor chart. In general, anchor charts have a single focus, and they reflect recent content or concepts that students need continued support in mastering. Anchor charts can provide reinforcement after students have learned classroom procedures and routines, how to handle transitions, the proper use of supplies and equipment, academic content, and social-emotional skills.

Here are some examples of anchor charts that may be useful in your classroom.

Ideas for Anchor Chart Topics

Topic	Anchor Chart Ideas
Procedures and Routines	• Turning in homework • Finding today's assignment • Recording upcoming school events in a planner
Transitions	• Entering the classroom late • Switching between small-group and whole-group work • Preparing to change classes
Proper Use of Supplies and Equipment	• Using and storing microscopes • Cleaning paintbrushes • Recharging batteries
Academic Content	• Scientific method • How to save a computer file • How to implement a math formula
Social-Emotional Skills	• Making eye contact • Resolving conflicts • Managing anger

Once students have mastered the content to the point where they no longer need a chart, it should be removed. When anchor charts are left up too long or when you have too many charts up, students may start ignoring them. You may wish to save charts for reposting later, such as for review or test preparation.

Anchor charts can be created by the teacher alone, but you may also find it helpful to co-create them with students. Doing so can keep students engaged and can be a good method in itself for reinforcing content. Interactive learning structures are useful for involving students in generating content for an anchor chart. Here's an example.

Maître d'

1. Name the learning goal. For example: "You're going to form different table sizes [standing groups] to share ideas about how to work with a lab partner."

2. Remind students about the expectations for forming new groups, emphasizing the importance of being inclusive, friendly, and respectful: "What will you do to make sure everyone is included?" (If needed, model how to move about the room safely.)

3. Call out a grouping, starting with "Table for two." Students quickly form pairs of their own choosing (with one table of three, if needed).

4. Ask a question to focus the discussion: "How can you work with your lab partner to make sure you're doing an experiment safely?" Give students 1–2 minutes to share (with a 15-second warning). Reinforce positive behavior: "I heard a lot of encouraging words when people got stuck on an idea to share."

5. Call out "Table for three," have students form new groups, and ask the same question or a new one, such as, "What are some things you can do to divide work up fairly with your lab partner?" After groups have discussed this question, call out "Table for four." Repeat as time allows, continuing to vary the table numbers.

6. Bring everyone back together and ask volunteers to share ideas from their conversations. Record these ideas on an anchor chart to post in a prominent place in the lab.

In addition to anchor charts, there are other supports you can use to reinforce content and help students stay on task. Table tents or mats placed right in the students' work area may provide a more immediate reminder of content. Timing devices—such as a large digital countdown timer for the class, or small sand timers that individual students or groups can use—can support students as they learn good time-management skills. Pay attention to where students need a little extra support, and look for anchors that can help them find that support independently.

Time Management

Many middle school students have after-school and extracurricular activities that compete with homework for their time. Introduce time-management planning this week to help students organize their time in a way that supports their achievement in school while helping them stay balanced, with adequate time for sleep and other basic needs.

When planning their after-school time, students should consider things such as:

- Homework

- Sports practice

- Family activities

- Time spent in transition (on the bus, in the car, walking)

- Meals

- Recreational activities (reading, doing creative projects, watching television)

- Taking care of siblings

- Household chores

- Socializing with friends (on their phone/computer or in person)

Here's an example of how students might use a time-management planner to help them manage their after-school and evening activities. After students complete their planners, suggest that they review them with a parent or guardian.

Time-Management Planner

Name: Rachel   Date: September 15

TIME	MONDAY	TUESDAY	WEDNESDAY	THURSDAY	FRIDAY
3:00	Study hall	Science club	Study hall	Band practice	Study hall
3:15					
3:30					
3:45	↓	↓	↓	↓	↓
4:00	Soccer	Soccer	Bus home	Soccer	Bus home
4:15			Chores		Chores
4:30			Homework		Television
4:45					
5:00					
5:15					↓
5:30	↓	↓		↓	Social media
5:45	Bus home	Bus home		Bus home	
6:00	Chores	Chores	↓	Chores	↓
6:15	Dinner	Dinner	Dinner	Dinner	Dinner
6:30	↓	↓	↓	↓	↓
6:45	Social media	Social media	Social media	Social media	Hang out with friends
7:00	Homework	Homework			Homework
7:15					
7:30					
7:45			↓		
8:00			Read		
8:15	↓	↓		↓	
8:30	Read	Read		Read	
8:45	↓	↓	↓	↓	↓
9:00	Go to bed	Go to bed	Go to bed	Go to bed	Go to bed

Download a printable Time-Management Planner template at
https://www.responsiveclassroom.org/printables/.

Brain Breaks

As you observe students and their interactions with each other, you will be able to gauge when they are ready for higher-risk activities. As they become more comfortable in the classroom community, incorporate brain breaks that are more complicated or that require students to share and participate with the whole group; take a social risk, like presenting an idea to the class; or involve a physical interaction, like shaking hands or giving a fist bump.

Refocusing Brain Break: Peaceful Reading

1. Have students stand by their desks, perform a few simple movements (stretching, jogging in place), then sit back down.

2. Choose a descriptive or peaceful poem or passage, and read it aloud. (Variation: Have students listen to a song or look at a painting or another piece of art for a few minutes.)

3. After the reading, invite a few student volunteers to discuss how they felt or what they visualized as they listened to the piece.

Recharging Brain Break: Do What I Said, Not What I Say

1. Have students stand at their desks or in a circle.

2. Explain to students that you will be calling out actions but that they must follow your previously given action, not the current one. (Consider having a student volunteer be the leader after you demonstrate how to do the activity for a few rounds.) Here's a sample set of leader instructions and student responses:

   - "Stand on one foot!" (students do nothing)

   - "Hop on one foot!" (students stand on one foot)

   - "Flap your arms!" (students hop on one foot)

   - "Pat your head!" (students flap their arms)

   - "Sit down!" (students pat their heads)

   - "Fold your hands on your desks!" (students sit down)

   - "Fold your hands on your desks!" (students fold their hands on their desks and are ready for the next lesson or activity)

Teaching Discipline

By week two, you should start to have a sense of who students are and where they may need support in demonstrating positive behavior. Keep enforcing the expectations you've laid out and showing students that you mean what you say. This week, you'll introduce additional strategies for responding to misbehavior.

Working With the Rules

In week one, students created SMART goals to give them a vision and direction to start off their school year. Now, in week two, it's time to use those SMART goals to get students invested in the classroom rules so that they have a personal stake in following those rules.

Remember: throughout their middle school years, students are deeply engaged in the important work of striving for independence and increased responsibility. This, coupled with their growing cognitive and reasoning skills, leads them to question and want to explore the boundaries of almost everything—from the meaning of words, to expectations for dress, to the rules in the classroom.

Connecting the rules to students' goals, learning, and community shows students that following the rules is about practicing self-control and self-discipline for one's own good and the good of the community, not about compliance or pleasing the teacher. This focus also helps to avoid reinforcing the notion that students who follow the rules are "teacher pleasers"—doing the right thing just to keep their teacher happy—while others may break the rules to challenge the teacher's authority.

Investing in the Rules

Investing students in the rules requires a proactive investment of time and effort in order to prevent misbehavior from happening. Although it may seem like a lot of time to take away from academics, this process saves a great deal of time and energy in the long run as it helps minimize misbehavior and makes classroom operations more productive and efficient.

As noted in week one, the process of investing students in the rules has four steps:

1. Setting SMART goals

2. Connecting goals to the rules

3. Connecting rules to concrete behavior

4. Making the rules come alive

With students' SMART goals set, week two picks up with steps two through four of the process. The goals of this collaborative process are:

- Create a shared vision of expectations and how the learning environment will support everyone's growth.

- Make explicit how each rule will look, sound, and feel when being followed.

- Build students' understanding of how their actions contribute to their success and to the success of others.

It may be helpful to spread the three remaining steps over multiple days this week to allow for reflection between class sessions.

Step 2: Connecting Goals to the Rules

Have students think about their goals as they consider the school or classroom rules. Give them a few minutes to write down specific ways in which the rules support their goals. For example:

- I want to get at least an A– in Spanish this quarter. Part of giving my best effort means taking good notes during class, which will help me do well on homework and tests.

- I want to find three new study partners this semester. Respecting others will help me get along with people so I can get to know them and ask them to study with me.

- I want to create an artist portfolio this year. Part of taking care of the classroom means keeping supplies organized and in good shape, which will help me create the pieces for my portfolio.

By connecting their goals to the rules, students are better able to see the rules as positive guidelines that help them achieve success and create the kind of community where everyone works together. Although students may not see how all the rules connect with their goals, they should see connections to at least one of the rules.

Once they've written down their connections, have a few volunteers share a connection. Try to find volunteers to share at least one goal for each rule. Emphasize that while any given student may not currently connect all the rules to their goals, each rule supports someone's goal. Thus, all the rules are important. Framing them as "our rules" further builds students' sense of ownership of the rules.

End this step with questions for students to reflect on before the next step. For example:

- What will you need from our community to achieve your goal?

- What are some ways that you can support each other to achieve your goals?

Step 3: Connecting Rules to Concrete Behavior

Because effective rules are global in nature and can be applied to many different situations, it's important to take time to discuss how those rules will actually look, sound, and feel when followed. Have students work in table groups or use an interactive learning structure like Maître d' (see page 70) to brainstorm ideas for how each classroom rule will look, sound, and feel in action. Once brainstorming is complete, have groups share their ideas, which you can record on an anchor chart for reference.

You might also come up with a number of scenarios and ask students, "How would each of our classroom rules apply to these situations?" For example:

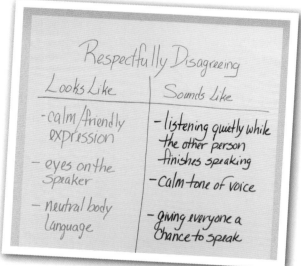

- A new student joins the class partway through the semester.

- We go on a field trip to an art museum.

- A glass beaker accidentally gets broken during a science experiment.

Encourage students to come up with ideas that go beyond the obvious. For instance, students might immediately say that they could follow the rule to "Respect the classroom space and materials" by cleaning up the broken glass beaker, but you might also prompt them to think about how they would apply the other rules. Perhaps they could "Take care of each other" by alerting others to the broken glass. Or, they might follow the rule "Do your best work" by staying focused after the glass has been cleaned up, continuing with their own experiment rather than getting distracted or chatting about the incident.

Step 4: Making the Rules Come Alive

The final step of the process involves integrating the rules into the daily life of the classroom on an ongoing basis. This step will continue throughout the year, and can include:

- Prominently displaying the rules in the classroom

- Frequently referring to the rules, both in reinforcing positive behavior and in offering reminders

- Revisiting the rules as needed, such as when new students join the class, after a holiday break or during a midyear slump, or when the class as a whole is struggling and could use a refresher

When reinforcing what students are doing well or giving proactive or reactive reminders, specifically reference the applicable rules. The following chart offers ideas for using teacher language that focuses on the rules rather than on the teacher and that fosters self-control and ethical, responsible behavior.

Using Teacher Language That Focuses on the Rules

Instead of a teacher-centered approach…	…use a rules-centered approach
"Liliana, I really appreciate how you helped Terrance when he got stuck on that math problem earlier."	"Liliana, you showed kindness when you helped Terrance with that math problem. You followed our rule 'Be a kind community member.'"
"It made me happy to see how well everyone took care of their musical instruments today."	"Everyone did such a great job following our rule 'Take care of classroom materials' today when you put away your instruments carefully."
"I'm going to be watching for students to walk respectfully in the halls to art class."	"One of our rules is 'Be respectful of others.' How might that look and sound as you walk past other classrooms to art?"
"I expect you all to be kind and respectful to Mr. Rodriguez when I'm in my meeting today."	"What are some specific ways you can follow our class rules when Mr. Rodriguez is here?"
"I'm getting very frustrated that people aren't focused on their writing conferences right now."	"Everyone, let's refocus. How can you follow our rule to 'Do your best work' right now during writing conferences?"

Logical Consequences

Along with investing students in the rules, this week is the time to teach them about the logical consequences of not following those rules. Just like adults, young adolescents may misbehave, whether on purpose or by accident, for a variety of reasons. They may be tired, hungry, angry, or frustrated. They may be trying to impress their friends or looking for attention. Or, they might simply be doing the normal developmental work of testing boundaries. No matter the reason, logical consequences can help them get their behavior back on task.

Even with the most effective classroom management and a strong sense of community, misbehavior will still happen. Just as students will make mistakes when learning a new language or doing math problems, they will make mistakes as they learn self-control and ethical behavior. These mistakes are a natural part of the learning process, and treating them as such can maintain positive teacher-student relationships and preserve students' dignity.

Logical consequences are a set of strategies for responding to misbehavior that allow the teacher to set clear limits and hold students to a high standard of behavior. These strategies are different from punishment, which uses external control to "make" students behave and often leaves students feeling angry, humiliated, resentful, or afraid. Logical consequences, on the other hand, focus on teaching students positive behavior skills so that they can develop self-control and the internal motivation to do right.

Logical consequences are:

- **Respectful**—Logical consequences focus on the student's behavior rather than their character; are given in a firm, calm manner; and do not interfere with the student's ability to learn.

- **Related**—Logical consequences directly relate to the misbehavior, and connect back to the classroom rules.

- **Realistic**—Logical consequences are things the student can reasonably do, and they do not put an undue burden on the teacher.

There are three types of logical consequences:

- **Loss of privilege**—When a student is having trouble handling the privilege of participating in an activity, working with a particular partner or group, or using materials, the privilege is briefly removed, usually for a class period or a day. For example, a student who keeps talking about movies instead of class content during a partner chat is required to switch partners or work alone for the rest of the activity.

- **Break it, fix it**—When a student breaks or damages something, whether on purpose or by accident, they help to fix it or clean it up. For example, a student who draws on their desk has to clean off what they drew.

- **Space and Time**—When a student has lost or is about to lose self-control, they step away for a few moments to a designated place to calm down and refocus. For example, a student who yells at a peer during a group activity has to go to the designated spot until they are able to regain self-control and speak in a respectful tone.

When introducing logical consequences to students, it's essential to talk about them as helpful tools rather than punishments. Focus on the true purpose of logical consequences: to help students practice self-control so that they can follow the class rules and meet their goals. Point out that we all make mistakes sometimes, and that we can all learn from them. It's helpful to mention some specific mistakes you've made, such as running out of time on a parking meter and getting a ticket, or spilling coffee on the floor of the staff break room that you then had to clean up. Students will benefit from seeing that you acknowledge your mistakes and take responsibility for fixing them.

Giving some examples of what logical consequences might look like in your classroom can help students better understand what to expect, which strengthens their sense of trust and safety in the classroom. By using common examples that every student can relate to, you will reinforce the idea that logical consequences apply to all students and that everyone will experience them at one time or another. Here are a few examples you could use:

Using Logical Consequences

Misbehavior	Applicable Rule	Logical Consequence
A student accidentally spills paint, and the paint splashes on another student's work.	Be respectful of our classroom materials.	Break it, fix it: The student cleans up the spilled paint and asks their classmate if they would like help fixing their work.
A student browses social media on a school tablet instead of using it for research.	Be ready to learn.	Loss of privilege: For today, the student needs to do their research with reference books instead of the tablet.
A student bothers a tablemate by hitting the table after that student has respectfully asked them to stop.	Be respectful of others.	Space and Time: The student needs to take a few moments away from the table to regain self-control.

Share these or other examples and have small groups of students discuss them together. To help students understand the process, you might also invite them to generate ideas for situations in which the consequence of break it, fix it might be applied, or ways in which privileges might be lost due to certain behavior. However, make it clear that in real-life instances of misbehavior, you'll be the one deciding on those logical consequences.

Space and Time is slightly different in that it is a specific procedure that needs to be modeled and practiced. Explain to students that just as the coach of a sports team might call a time-out when a player isn't doing their best, you might call time-out and send a student to Space and Time to help them get ready to return to learning. Because some students may have experienced a punitive form of time-out in the past, it's important to emphasize that in this classroom, Space and Time is simply a way to regain self-control.

Use Interactive Modeling (see pages 6–7) to demonstrate how to calmly and quietly go to a designated spot for taking Space and Time, how to behave while there, and how to rejoin the rest of the class afterward. You might also model some techniques student can use to cool down while they're in Space and Time, such as deep breathing, stretching, or meditation.

Over the course of the week, give every student at least one opportunity to practice taking Space and Time, always during moments when they are in control and following the rules. It's helpful to keep a running log of who has practiced to make sure everyone has a chance. You may also choose to use Space and Time yourself to let students see that adults, too, sometimes need to step away from an activity to refocus. This is a great way to debunk the idea that the Space and Time area is a place for students who are "bad" and show it for what it is—a place to find self-control.

Tips for using Space and Time:

- Give a few specific options for places to take Space and Time, such as an empty desk where a student can sit or a spot by the window where they can stand and stretch. Make sure the designated areas are separate enough from the rest of the class to give the student the distance they need but close enough that they can still follow along with instruction and make a smooth transition back into the flow of learning. The purpose of Space and Time is not to isolate the student but to allow them and the class as a whole to productively continue learning.

- Choose what to call Space and Time. In some classrooms, it's called "take-a-break," "rest stop," or another name. It may be helpful to coordinate with your team or even the school as a whole to use a consistent name so that students understand how to use this practice throughout the school.

- Keep your voice, facial expression, and body language calm and neutral when you instruct students to take Space and Time, and tell them as discreetly as possible to avoid embarrassment and power struggles. If necessary, take a moment to take a deep breath before sending them so that you're able to stay calm and maintain empathy.

- Early on, signal students to rejoin the class once they've had a few minutes to refocus and you sense they're ready to come back. Later, teach students how to interpret their own physical and emotional signals so that they can decide for themselves when to come back. This gives them autonomy and helps them build self-awareness and self-control.

- After students are familiar with using Space and Time, let them go on their own when they feel themselves losing self-control.

- Teach the class to stay focused on their own work when a classmate is in Space and Time. Emphasize the importance of respecting both their classmate's privacy and their own learning.

- Use Space and Time at the first sign that a student is losing control. This will make it easier for the student to regain control than it will be if you wait until their behavior has escalated to a full-blown outburst.

- Make sure students see that Space and Time is for everyone, not just the same few students. We all have times when we get frustrated, have trouble concentrating, or act out—and it's helpful to all of us to develop the skill of recognizing these moments and take time to regain self-control.

Week Three

If you're making mistakes, it means you're out there doing something. And the mistakes in themselves can be useful.

—Neil Gaiman, writer

By the third week of school, the classroom community is growing stronger. We may observe students following routines more reliably and autonomously, and there is an air of familiarity as students get to know each other within and outside your classroom. Even if students were in class together the year before, there is more for them to learn about each other due to the rapid changes of young adolescence, including new interests, identity formation, cognitive development, and ethical reasoning. You, too, have likely started to notice the individual strengths, needs, and diverse personalities present in your classroom community.

Goals for Week Three

As your class gains momentum, this week's goals provide opportunities for students to further strengthen their relationships with you and with one another, and to experience the right level of academic challenge for them.

1. **Continue building a positive classroom community.** By week three, the class will likely have taken on a life of its own. Continue to give students daily opportunities to work cooperatively, state opinions respectfully, wait their turn, practice routines, and socialize responsibly. All of these elements add up to a safe, well-managed classroom where students feel connected and supported in taking academic risks.

2. **Use instructional practices that build academic and social-emotional skills for success.** The teaching strategies you choose can help students stay engaged with academics and can also support social-emotional learning. Interactive learning structures that allow for learning through social interaction can help students practice and apply both academic and social-emotional skills, and are an important way to meet middle school students' unique needs.

3. **Provide an appropriate amount of academic challenge.** When you challenge students to push themselves academically, you communicate that you respect them, want them to succeed, and believe they can succeed. By week three, you'll be well on your way to understanding students personally and academically, and this foundation will allow you to provide appropriate academic challenges and set the expectation that students will work hard to meet those challenges.

4. **Recognize and respond to chronic misbehavior and emotional outbursts.** Students come to school with a variety of stressors. Observe students over the first few weeks of school to see which of them may struggle with toxic stress or chronic behavior issues, and what factors may trigger outbursts or shutting down. Use these observations to make a plan for dealing with these behaviors, and work on understanding what it means when a student is in fight, flight, or freeze mode and how to help them calm down and get back in control of themselves.

Creating Conditions for Success

During the middle school years, students begin to experience an increasingly demanding academic load. They are often engaged in academic work that requires a greater degree of independence, yet their need for social interaction remains very high. In order to keep students engaged in academics, it is imperative to implement lessons and strategies that allow for healthy, productive social interactions while meeting the expectations for academics.

Building Community

By the third week of school, students will be starting to produce work that can be displayed or showcased in your classroom. Displaying this work shows that you value each student's contributions and sends the message that this classroom is a community where everyone can learn from one another. Consider the following tips for displaying student work:

- Every student who wishes to participate should have work on display. While you won't display every piece of work students do, everyone should be represented at any given time. If a student does not wish to have their work on display, talk to them about why. Are they not yet feeling comfortable with their peers? Do they lack confidence in this subject area? Help them find ways to overcome these challenges so that they will feel ready to showcase their work when you put up a new display.

- Ask for input from students. Students must have a say in what you display, and not all students need to have the same work displayed. Consider creating displays that showcase a variety of topics and projects going on in the class.

- Display work in progress as well as finished products. This reflects the belief that the process is as important as the product, and can help students see that their work doesn't have to be perfect to be worthy of showcasing.

- Keep displays fresh. After work has been up for a couple of weeks, students generally stop looking at it. Swap in new work to reflect new units of study and students' developing skills.

Responsive Advisory Meeting

In week three, continue to introduce more in-depth Responsive Advisory Meeting components as you sense students' readiness for higher-risk activities. This week, you might choose to focus Responsive Advisory Meeting on the theme of developing communication and social skills to help students continue deepening their connections with one another and prepare them to successfully work together in group discussions and collaborative projects. Here are a few ideas you might include in Responsive Advisory Meeting this week.

Arrival Welcome

Stand at the door and welcome students by name as they enter. Consider adding a fist bump or high five.

Announcements

Hello, Communicators!

Have you heard the saying "Let's agree to disagree"? It's when two or more opposing sides come to an agreement that they disagree on a topic and therefore will stop trying to convince the other side. For example: Joe thinks baseball is the best sport, but Mariana says soccer is the best, so they agree to disagree. Think about some times when it might be necessary to respectfully agree to disagree.

Acknowledgments

Have each student write down one word related to respect (for example, "kindness," "empathy," "listening"). In their table group, students work together to create one sentence or paragraph using all their words. Each group shares their sentence or paragraph with the whole class.

Activity

Carousel: Post chart paper around the room. Label each sheet with one of the following topics:

- Disagree with project partner on presentation topic
- Disagree with teacher about project deadline
- Disagree with parents about chores
- Disagree with friend about whose house to go to

Have students count off by fours, give each group a different colored marker, and assign each group to one of the topics. Each group brainstorms positive ways to address both sides of the disagreement and records their ideas on the chart. On your signal, groups rotate to the next chart and add to the listed ideas. Keep things moving by shortening rotation times as the process continues. Conclude once all groups have visited all charts.

 To close the meeting, ask students a reflection question: "Think about a disagreement you've had with someone. What new ideas do you have for how you could handle a future disagreement?"

 Download a printable Responsive Advisory Meeting Planning Guide at https://www.responsiveclassroom.org/printables/.

Teacher Language

The *Responsive Classroom* approach strives to help students become intrinsically motivated to behave in ways that enable them to be socially and academically successful. However, just like all of us, adolescents still need to feel recognized and encouraged for their positive efforts, contributions, and accomplishments. Reinforcing language helps students develop intrinsic motivation because it provides specific feedback on what they're doing right, which students can then use to shape future behavior.

During this week, take a few minutes to do a self-check on how you're progressing with using reinforcing language. As part of your reflection, consider what you're doing that keeps you moving toward your teacher language goals, and identify any distractions or difficulties that may be obstacles to reaching your goals.

Transitions and Nonclassroom Spaces

The key to smooth transitions is good management—of time, social interactions (including conflicts), stress, and emotions. Helping students envision what respectful peer interactions look and sound like can guide their actions during times when they have little supervision. Monitor students in the hallways, at the beginning and end of class periods, and during and after lunch, and think about where they might still need support in developing the skills they need to behave responsibly.

Graphic organizers are one way to help students envision and achieve respectful behavior in these areas. A graphic organizer is a visual tool students can use to express their thinking and knowledge, grasp of concepts and ideas, and understanding of the relationships among them. Using graphic organizers to help students think about transitions is a strategy you can use now and return to throughout the school year as needed.

On the following pages, you'll find three types of graphic organizers to try: Looks Like, Sounds Like, Feels Like; Cause and Effect; and Decision Tree. All of these graphic organizers can be used with students throughout middle school for academic or social-emotional topics, but here are some specific ways to tailor them to students' developmental needs as you work with them on smooth transitions.

 Download printable graphic organizer templates at
https://www.responsiveclassroom.org/printables/.

Sixth Graders

As the newest arrivals to middle school, sixth graders may be just starting to develop the skills they need to thrive in this new setting and may be feeling overwhelmed or stressed. As you observe students, pay attention to the changes they may be struggling with the most. A tool such as **Looks Like, Sounds Like, Feels Like** can help students gain perspective and form an empowering image of what they can do to calm themselves, get to class on time, or handle social pressures.

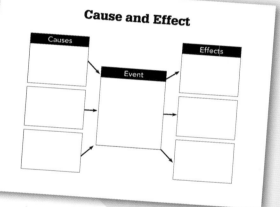

Seventh Graders

Characteristic of their emerging independence, seventh graders want to contribute to their own solutions for managing transitions. They have a strong sense of right and wrong and a desire to strive for democratic ideals such as fairness, equality, and justice. The **Cause and Effect** graphic organizer shows relationships between events, allowing learners to think about the consequences their actions may have. This tool can be used to explore social interactions, academic strategies, and how personal and larger actions may affect individuals and the community.

Eighth Graders

Eighth graders are focused on developing their identities as individuals and as members of a group. Giving them opportunities to concretely identify how they make good choices can help them grow in confidence as people who do the right thing. Creating a **Decision Tree** is an effective and quick strategy for helping them safely examine the possible outcomes of different decisions, whether academic or social.

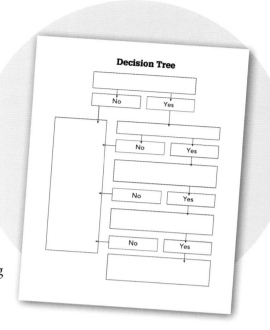

There are a number of ways to provide scaffolding to help students work with graphic organizers. For example, you could:

- Guide students through a visualization to help them paint a mental picture

- Ask prompting questions

- Use anchor charts to show key points

- Have students discuss ideas in small groups

- Brainstorm possible ideas

Closing the School Day

Each student brings their own personality, interests, and social history to the classroom. It is our job to bring this eclectic mix of students together into a cohesive and cooperative community. One way to encourage this process is by reinforcing a positive class identity as it starts to emerge. Naming positive attributes you see in the classroom community can help instill a sense of group pride and positive connections among students. Remember to stay focused on what the class is doing right—not what they're doing better than others. The goal is to develop a shared sense of identity rather than a sense of competition or superiority.

During week three, you might choose to cultivate a sense of shared identity by reflecting on and celebrating individual, class, or team accomplishments while closing the day. You can also use this time to reinforce essential communication skills, such as speaking clearly and actively listening to others' perspectives with tolerance and respect.

You might guide the discussion with one of these prompts:

- Name one thing that went well in our classroom or school community today.

- What's one thing you look forward to tomorrow?

- Name one thing you did today to contribute to a positive classroom or school experience.

- What is one way you took care of or advocated for yourself today?

- Name one example of how you or another person showed kindness today.

- Name one way you took the perspective of another person.

- What is one thing we can all do to help our school be a welcoming place for everyone?

- What is one strategy you used to be successful today?

- What is one way you helped someone today?

- What is a positive experience you had today that you'd like to try again tomorrow?

- What is one way our class followed the rules today?

Working With Your Team

As the early weeks of school progress, keep meeting with your team to determine what's working and brainstorm ideas for getting past obstacles. Continue coordinating with your teammates on activities and interactive learning structures to keep things fresh and avoid too much repetition. Some other ideas for discussion with your teammates this week:

- Create a schedule for showcasing student work. This might involve staggering dates by topic or class period. You might even create a plan of showcasing different steps of the same task to show the learning process. No matter how you organize this schedule, make sure that students have a say in which work they display.

- Discuss how everyone is doing with closing the day. It may be useful to coordinate topics or activities, creating a framework that everyone can follow in the next few weeks. Or, the team could share how they've used this practice in ways they've found meaningful.

- Discuss ways in which academics will become more challenging this week. Talk about how to help students manage these challenges, as well as how to help them continue to practice social and communication skills.

Teaching Academics

As you move into week three, the stronger sense you're gaining of students' social-emotional and academic strengths and areas for growth can help you meet this week's goal to provide an appropriate amount of academic challenge. This week, show that you have high expectations for all the students in your classroom, no matter where their starting point may be. They will rise to the occasion when you show that you believe they can meet those high expectations and you give them the tools and the practice time they need.

As students dig deeper into academic content, it's important to find ways to help them maintain the energy they brought to the classroom at the beginning of the year. The strategies this week can be used now and throughout the year to keep students active and focused. These strategies appeal to young adolescents' developmental needs and work with their natural tendencies to make the most of learning.

Interactive Learning Structures

This week, pay special attention to the social and emotional skills students will practice when using interactive learning structures. For example, a structure such as the one that follows can help students not only explore academic content but also build their skills in cooperation, empathy, assertiveness, and self-control.

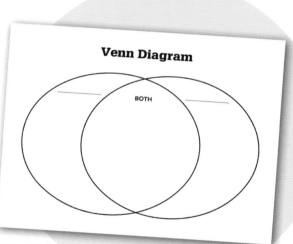

Venn-ting

1. Name the learning goal. For example: "You'll be exploring the similarities and differences between poetry and fiction."

2. Pair students and have them decide who will be the reporter and who will be the presenter. Remind students about the importance of cooperation: "Name some ways you can ensure that both partners' ideas are included."

3. Have each pair set up a Venn diagram and label the two circles with the two topics you mentioned. The sections on the sides will contain ideas that apply to only one of the topics, and the overlapping section in the center will contain ideas that apply to both.

4. State the number of similarities and differences students should try to identify. Give them 3–5 minutes to brainstorm ideas (with a 30-second warning before time's up).

5. The reporter from each pair then roams the room looking at other diagrams. The presenter stays put and explains their work to the other reporters. Allow reporters to visit two or three different diagrams and stay for 1–2 minutes at each.

6. Reporters return to their original partners and discuss what they learned. Give students a few minutes to add to or revise their original diagrams. Reinforce positive behavior: "People were listening respectfully as others shared their ideas. That helps everyone expand their thinking."

 Download a printable Venn Diagram template at https://www.responsiveclassroom.org/printables/.

Active Teaching

Although lecturing while students take notes is a common strategy for teaching, more effective strategies for middle school students are those that play to their developmental strengths and need for activity, social interaction, and fun. Active teaching is a straightforward, developmentally appropriate strategy for delivering instruction to middle school students that consists of three phases: teach and model, student collaboration, and facilitate reflection. During this process, the teacher presents, explains, illustrates, and demonstrates content in a way that enables students to meet a learning objective that clearly describes what students should know, understand, and be able to do.

Before beginning this active teaching, we need to do three things: make connections to relevant prior knowledge or skills, explicitly describe what students will learn and should be able to do at the end of the lesson or unit (up to and including a summative evaluation), and help students make a personal connection to the learning. After these preliminary steps have been completed, we can move into the three phases of active teaching.

Phase 1: Teach and Model

The teach and model phase involves presenting content in a way that excites students and makes them curious to learn more. Rather than simply lecturing, this type of teaching incorporates demonstrations and open-ended questions that allow students to engage more deeply with the content. During this phase, we also make significant use of models—either those that are ready to use or that we create in advance, or those that students create as part of our teaching. Consider the following sorts of tools:

- **Graphic organizers** like the ones introduced on pages 88–90, which allow students to visualize ideas and the connections between them.

- **Physical models,** which enable students to engage in hands-on learning and develop stronger mental images by creating concrete representations of what they're learning. Examples include flash cards, maps, board games, math manipulatives, and scientific models.

- **Mental images,** which use emotions and the five senses to create a picture in students' minds of content and skills being learned. These images may be generated through the use of guided visualization, mnemonic devices, partner discussions, analogies, or other techniques.

- **Pictures and pictographs** created by students, which allow them to form their own visual representations of their knowledge and understanding. They may draw, paint, or use technology to create illustrations, infographics, videos, comics, or other still or moving images.

- **Kinesthetic activities,** which help students solidify and demonstrate their understanding through movement. These could include charades, curriculum-related brain breaks, role-plays, or other movement-based activities.

Phase 2: Student Collaboration

During this phase, students gather in pairs or small groups to discuss what they noticed and learned about the content you presented during the teach and model phase. You could have them focus, for example, on the specific steps of a process, a key content point you highlighted, or a particular technique you modeled. By giving them the opportunity and responsibility for noticing and reacting to the details of your teaching, you demonstrate to students that their ideas matter. This creates a sense of importance and belonging that, combined with opportunities to talk and listen, naturally leads to more engagement and learning retention.

This kind of student collaboration does not happen automatically in a classroom. We have to nurture it through the use of four key strategies:

- **Provide a structure for students' collaborative conversations**—The goal of student collaboration is for students to share and deepen their understanding of the content. Interactive learning structures, such as the ones throughout this book, can provide clear expectations for these conversations. When preparing to use these structures, set students up for success by reminding them of or modeling the skills they will need to effectively collaborate with each other.

- **Jump-start students' thinking with questions or sentence stems**—Content-centered conversations may not happen spontaneously. Students need to be taught how to engage in academic conversations with their classmates, and we can scaffold productive conversations using questions and sentence stems. For example, after teaching how to do a scientific procedure, you might ask, "Why is it important to follow this sequence? What would happen if you went out of sequence?" You might then provide a sentence stem to help students think through the question: "I can see how completing each step in order would help me _____."

- **Model giving and receiving constructive comments**—When students work collaboratively, they need to be able to give and receive constructive feedback. Students need to be explicitly taught what it looks, sounds, and feels like to ask for clarification, agree or disagree with a comment, add on to a comment, respond to disagreement, and get the group back on course when the conversation goes off topic.

- **Remind students of the expectations for small group learning**—Because students work together during this phase, make sure they remember the expectations for working in groups. Use reminding language as needed to prompt them to recall effective communication skills you've taught them, ways to productively divide tasks, and any other skills needed for the activities at hand.

Phase 3: Facilitate Reflection

Teacher-facilitated reflection helps ensure that students make meaning of their learning by thinking about how they experienced that learning. You may be able to recall an experience in which you were learning something new that you couldn't grasp right away, but after having some time to process or reflect, you got it. The same is true for students: Reflection helps them solidify what they've learned and understand how they've learned it.

Many of us think of reflection as a quiet, solitary act. But reflection also takes place when students engage in teacher-facilitated conversation with peers. Students don't naturally know how to do this kind of reflection, but by practicing with your help, they will develop the necessary skills to become reflective learners.

Remember that reflection is not the same as recounting or restating knowledge, such as what students would do when taking a quiz. Showing mastery of content in that way is important, but the purposes of reflection are different. Through reflection, students become more aware of how they learn. They reflect on the strategies they used and think about ways to adapt those strategies for use in the future. Reflection also helps students take more responsibility for their own learning rather than seeing it as something they're doing for others or something that's being done to them. Finally, reflection allows students to see growth in their own learning rather than waiting to be told by a test. Guiding students to think about themselves as learners—to take notice of their starting point at the beginning of direct teaching and to assess their progress as the teaching continues—helps them see their own strengths and their ability to learn and grow.

Asking reflection questions such as the following can help guide students' thinking. You could use these as small-group or whole-class discussion prompts, writing or art activity prompts, or (depending on the resources available) topics for social media activities and digital portfolios.

- **Help students become more aware of how they learn**
  - What class activities or tasks did you do that helped you learn the most?
  - What skills or strategies did you use to help you learn the content?
  - What supports might have helped you meet this objective more easily?
  - What's one thing you liked about how this content was taught? Why?

- **Help students take more responsibility for their learning**
  - If you could do this over, what would you do differently to improve your performance?
  - What did you do that contributed to your learning today?
  - Which aspects of your efforts do you think contributed the most to your success in meeting the objective?
  - What part of the learning do you feel most unsure of? What do you think would help you become more sure?
  - Why do you think this learning objective is important?
- **Help students see growth in their learning**
  - How can you prove that you met the learning objective? What evidence do you have to support your response?
  - What did you learn today (this week)?
  - What do you know about this content now that you didn't know before?

Active teaching can be used across the curriculum and in all courses. The following chart features an example of a science lesson that makes use of active teaching.

Using Active Teaching

Teach and model	The teacher delivers a lesson on identifying the steps of the water cycle. She uses models to help students understand each step. For example, she shows an animation of water vapor escaping a body of water into the atmosphere to illustrate evaporation.
Student collaboration	The teacher instructs students to work with their table partners to create their own visual of the steps of the water cycle. Before they begin work, she asks, "What are some ways you can handle a disagreement if there are multiple ideas for creating your visual?"
Facilitate reflection	The teacher asks students to reflect on what knowledge they needed to create their visual, and how creating the visual will help them remember the steps involved in the water cycle. Students structure these reflections as a journal entry.

Student Practice

Student practice immediately follows and goes hand in hand with active teaching. Under the teacher's watchful guidance, students try out the content and skills they just learned during active teaching. Student practice is an opportunity for teachers to identify and correct errors in students' thinking before setting them free to practice further on their own. It's also a natural time to increase students' motivation for taking on challenging work.

Student practice validates the perspective that practice leads to mastery. It encourages students to try out new ways of thinking, take small steps that yield visible results, and use new resources to support these steps. Practice is done in the safety of a small group, which feeds young adolescents' craving for social interaction, and is deliberately structured to be fun and appropriately challenging.

For student practice to be most effective, teachers need to take three key actions. These actions are not necessarily sequential; teachers can use them in a fluid way.

- **Remind students of the learning objective**—Restate the objective you noted during the first phase of active teaching. Use envisioning language that presents a clear and engaging picture of what is possible for students as they deepen their learning and that elevates practice over performance.

- **Structure and focus meaningful practice**—Make student practice collaborative, and bring a sense of playful exploration to it to help students engage more deeply. During student practice, the teacher is still there to guide and help facilitate, but students have a sense of independence as they build their knowledge base. Use reinforcing language to recognize students' successful use of skills, display of positive attitudes, and choice of productive work processes or strategies.

- **Use formative assessments to determine readiness**—Before moving on to independent practice, use formative assessments to reflect on the effectiveness of your

Avoid grading students during student practice

Although student practice is an opportunity for students to react to our active teaching, it is not the time to put a final stamp on their efforts in the form of a grade. Grading students' early efforts during student practice may result in their forming fixed mindsets. Instead, give students opportunities to play around with the new content. Even formative assessments done during student practice are intended only to inform our decision-making about what supports students may need: Should we stop and reteach something? Would an anchor chart help students solidify their learning?

instructional delivery and to make informed, confident decisions about whether one, some, or all students need reteaching or are sufficiently prepared to be released to independent work. Formative assessments can be as simple as observing students or asking them to give a thumbs-up or thumbs-down to help you gauge their understanding, or they can include more detailed written assessments, quizzes, or oral responses. Use diagnostic questions to help you check students' thinking, such as "What led you to think that?" "Can you think of another example of this?" or "Would this answer always apply, or only under certain conditions?" If your diagnostic questions or other formative assessments tell you that students have misconceptions or are foggy about any part of the content, stop and reteach before asking students to move to independent practice. Otherwise, they'll be practicing—and solidifying—mistakes and misconceptions.

In order to keep student practice meaningful, fun, and engaging, choose highly focused, well-structured activities. These qualities will help ensure that students:

- Show a high degree of effort

- Find the work challenging

- Have intrinsic motivation to do the work

- Experience positive relationships with one another

- Find learning enjoyable

Consider the following questions when planning activities for student practice.

High Focus

- Do I focus students' attention on the learning objective before I do direct teaching?

- Do I notice students becoming increasingly comfortable with collaboration during my direct teaching?

- Do I give students regular opportunities to reflect on their learning?

- Do students' responses to my formative assessments give me a clear indication of whether to reteach or move on?

- Do I regularly reinforce effort through guided practice prior to releasing students to independent practice?

Well-Designed Structures

- Do students appropriately use anchoring supports for partner chats and table talks?

- Do I consistently give focused directions before students engage in interactive learning structures?

- Am I using Interactive Modeling to teach students exactly what to do?

- Am I consistently using reinforcing language to help students recognize when they demonstrate specific social and academic skills that support success in school?

Brain Breaks

As the school year gets up to full speed, make regular use of brain breaks to keep students energized and ready to learn. If you sense that students are starting to feel the pressure of academics and getting stressed out, try a refocusing brain break. Or if energy is flagging due to the time of day or a long period of sitting still, try a quick recharging brain break.

Refocusing Brain Break: Mellow Echo

1. Students stand or sit at their desks. The leader performs slow motions, poses, or stretches while naming them. Students echo what the leader says while imitating the motions. For example: "Breathe in and lift your arms up" (lift arms up); "Breathe out and let your arms drift down" (let arms drift down).

2. The leader continues with other calming motions for students to follow.

3. Conclude with a few deep breaths in and out.

Recharging Brain Break: Ma Zinga

1. Students stand in a circle, with their arms pointing straight into the middle of the circle (or stand by their desks and point toward the front of the room). Choose a student to be the leader or ask for a volunteer.

2. The group says "Ma-a-a-a . . ." with the "ah" sound gradually rising as students shake their fingers, hands, and arms to build up energy and a sense of team spirit.

3. At the leader's signal—a nod of the head—the group quickly pulls back their hands while forming fists and cheering "Zinga!" loudly together. This motion pulls all that great team spirit and energy back into each individual.

4. Repeat with a new leader as time allows.

Teaching Discipline

This week, keep building the classroom and school community by being consistent in keeping the rules alive and showing students that you will hold them to the expectations you've set. As you get to know students better, you'll begin to have a stronger sense of what they need in order to be successful in your classroom.

Working With the Rules

Last week, you went through the process of investing students in the rules. This week and throughout the year, continue with the fourth step of that process and make the rules come alive. One way to do this is to phrase reminders as prompting questions related to a current activity or transition. For example:

- When the class is getting ready to leave for lunch: "What are some ways we can follow the rules in the cafeteria?"

- As the class prepares to do online research: "When you're doing your research, how can you follow our rule to 'Show your best effort'?"

- Before a longer, more in-depth activity begins: "How might you 'Take care of yourself' and 'Take care of each other' if you're having a partner discussion and it starts to get off topic?"

When referring to the rules, avoid adding consequences to your reminder. That way, students' motivation for following the rules isn't to avoid the consequence but to meet the expectations of the community and work toward their own goals. Regularly referring to class rules sends a clear message: "We are all striving to live up to the ideals we've set for ourselves in all areas of our school life together."

Responding to Misbehavior

This week, continue to communicate with your team about any behavior issues that are cropping up. Discuss how reminding and redirecting language, teacher cues, and logical consequences are working, and identify any students who are experiencing more persistent problem behavior. By this point in the school year, you may start to become aware of students who are more prone to serious outbursts or who shut down or run off in the face of stressful situations. Talk to your colleagues about strategies that have been successful for working with these students, and consider whether toxic stress may be a factor in these students' lives.

Dealing With Toxic Stress and Emotional Outbursts

All of us experience stress sometimes, but for students who have experienced serious trauma, stress can have a profound impact on their lives. These students may come from any background and may experience the phenomenon known as toxic stress from a variety of ongoing stressors, such as physical or emotional abuse or neglect, a parent's addiction, or regular exposure to violence in their community.

In times of stress, one's cortisol and other stress hormones rise, as do blood pressure and heart rate. When stressful moments are frequent and these hormones are elevated more regularly, they can negatively affect young adolescents' brains and other organs and prime students to go into "fight, flight, or freeze" mode much more easily. And when students are in this mode, they are physiologically unable to fully engage with learning and may engage in outbursts or withdrawal. At these times, the primary goals must be to help the student calm down and maintain their safety and the safety of everyone around them.

Although outbursts may be frustrating and disruptive, it's essential to handle them with care and compassion. Harsh punitive approaches, such as suspension, may only exacerbate the problem, as they don't address the student's underlying needs. In addition, removing students from school can cause them to fall behind in their academic work, leading to more frustration and, thus, to more outbursts. Mishandling these incidents can also create a tense or an uncertain classroom environment, where all students feel unsafe. The following tips offer insights on how to handle incidents in a way that is as peaceful, productive, and safe as possible for everyone involved.

- During calm moments, observe students who have experienced outbursts or who have shut down. See if you can identify situations that increase their stress and warning signs that an outburst or withdrawal is imminent.

- Use visual cues, teacher proximity, or even a customized signal to help a student regain self-control when you sense that they are struggling. You might also give the student the opportunity to take Space and Time (assuming you've fully established it as a nonpunitive practice) or to go for a brief walk down the hall and back if they need a moment to collect themselves. Knowing students as individuals will help you recognize what they need in the moment.

- When an outburst happens, the most important first step is to regain control of the situation and make sure the student and everyone else in the classroom is safe.

This may require moving the student to a different space or distracting them from the situation, whichever is most effective.

- Maintain a calm demeanor and use as few words as possible in the heat of the moment. Make sure your tone is sincere so students know you genuinely want to help. During an outburst, keep focused on restoring calm to the student and the class, and reserve any discussions about the incident until later on, when the student has resumed being able to focus on a rational conversation.

- Remember that it's essential to maintain empathy in order to truly help a student who's having an outburst. Try not to take these incidents personally. Using kind language and dealing with incidents as privately as possible will help students trust you, which can lead to an increased sense of rapport that may help minimize future outbursts. If you find that you are struggling to be empathetic toward a student who is having an outburst, it's time to have a teammate, a guidance counselor, or another adult take over for the moment until you, too, can cool down.

- After the moment of an outburst has passed and the student has regained control, speak to them privately, kindly, and nonjudgmentally about what happened, and ask for their input. Doing so can not only help you better understand the student's triggers and warning signs but also help them learn the essential skill of putting their feelings into words—an ability many students experiencing toxic stress struggle with and need support in developing. Ask, too, what support the student feels would help them avoid outbursts or shutting down and regain self-control in the future.

In addition to dealing with outbursts and withdrawal in a safe and respectful way, it's important to build a foundation of support for students experiencing toxic stress. The *Responsive Classroom* approach to helping these students is built on six pillars:

1. Provide an emotionally safe school and classroom

2. Model respectfulness

3. Explicitly teach social and emotional skills

4. Incorporate playfulness into learning

5. Communicate hope

6. Foster your own self-care and build a supportive community

With each of these pillars comes a set of strategies you can use in the classroom to build a foundation of support. Combined, these pillars can help you create a safe and healthy environment in which students can succeed academically and build critical social and emotional skills.

1. Provide an Emotionally Safe School and Classroom

The work you've done so far this year to build the classroom and school community is a good start to helping students experiencing toxic stress feel more at ease and ready to participate in learning. Here are some ways to continue toward that goal:

- Continue to forge strong, respectful connections with students and between students and their peers through Responsive Advisory Meeting, closing the day, and other opportunities for collaboration.

- Regularly incorporate refocusing brain breaks into the class period.

- Continue using Interactive Modeling throughout the school year when introducing new procedures or skills, or when you sense students need a reminder. Providing clear instructions and expectations helps students feel a sense of predictability and safety in the classroom.

- Be a good listener, and let students know you're available if they need to talk to you. Demonstrate your trustworthiness by finding distraction-free places to talk, where a student can have some privacy. Ask open-ended questions to encourage students to express themselves, and maintain a calm and kind tone of voice and relaxed, neutral body language that shows that you're listening.

2. Model Respectfulness

Building a climate of respect is important for the success and well-being of all students, but particularly those experiencing toxic stress. Young adolescents who experience toxic stress may be more likely than others to interpret innocent interactions as disrespectful, and they may act out when they're feeling disrespected. Thus, displaying respect toward students and encouraging them to act respectfully toward one another can help those experiencing toxic stress feel calmer, more comfortable, and less likely to go into fight, flight, or freeze mode. Here are some other ways to model and cultivate an atmosphere of respectfulness:

- Give students an appropriate level of academic challenge and the autonomy to complete their work. By doing so, you show students that you believe in their capability to succeed.

- Use reinforcing language to convey to students what you see them doing well, and use reminding language to show that you believe in their ability to stay on task and make good decisions.

- Teach the skills needed for cooperation, and allow students ample opportunities to work together and practice these skills. In particular, help students learn and practice how to resolve conflicts peacefully, work with peers toward a common goal, and work through obstacles, like having a difference of opinion or getting stuck on a problem.

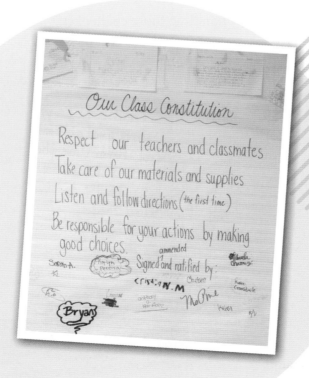

3. Explicitly Teach Social and Emotional Skills

Since young adolescents experiencing toxic stress are prone to easily going into fight, flight, or freeze mode, they need extra practice in controlling their impulses. Fortunately, the classroom provides many opportunities for teaching and practicing self-control, which allows students to regulate their thoughts, emotions, and behaviors. Here are some ways to teach social and emotional skills and help students practice self-control:

- Use visual cues and teacher proximity to let students know you're paying attention and to show them you believe in their ability to meet the expectations they've been taught.

- Use logical consequences to give students a blueprint for what self-control looks like. By having students take Space and Time when they need to calm down, guiding them to fix something they've broken, or removing a privilege that isn't being used responsibly, you show them how to get back on task, and you teach students strategies to help them be more successful next time. (Note: Logical consequences may not always be the optimal strategy for addressing misbehavior, particularly for students experiencing toxic stress. If the situation has escalated beyond ordinary misbehavior to the point of being a full-blown outburst, see pages 102–103 for strategies to try.)

- Help students talk about, identify, and label their feelings and express their emotions through healthy outlets, such as writing in a journal or drawing.

- Work with students to anticipate challenges they may face in upcoming projects, and help them brainstorm ideas for handling those challenges.

- Teach students skills they can use when their stress begins to rise, such as meditation techniques, positive self-talk, and tactile grounding techniques, like running their hands under cold water. Discuss appropriate techniques for using at one's desk, while taking Space and Time, or in other areas.

4. Incorporate Playfulness Into Learning

While the learning students do in the classroom is serious and important work, bringing a spirit of playfulness to that work can help students feel more comfortable, open, and creative. Playfulness thrives when we foster low-risk competition, shared engagement, friendly conversation, and opportunities to demonstrate a sense of humor. Since playfulness is malleable—a mood rather than a fixed personality characteristic—we can encourage it in students experiencing toxic stress to help them feel a stronger sense of belonging, significance, and fun and engage more deeply in the learning community. Here are some ways to incorporate playfulness into the life of your classroom:

- Use brain breaks to give students a chance to relax and enjoy themselves with their peers. If some students are reluctant to participate, find lower-risk ways to include them, such as by having them turn the lights off during a quiet activity or simply observe and then share what they saw. This type of indirect involvement may pave the way for students to feel more comfortable fully participating next time.

- Maintain a sense of humor by being willing to laugh at yourself and find the humor in challenging situations, as appropriate. Also, find the lighthearted side of your academic content by using (or having students create) riddles or jokes that incorporate history facts, scientific terms, or vocabulary words.

- Encourage creative play through skits, dance, songs, drawings, and other such activities, or have students create a board game or comic strip about a topic they're studying.

- Play on students' natural inquisitiveness. Build excitement by having students follow their own curiosity as they do science experiments, explore the library, or do research.

5. Communicate Hope

Hope is more than wishful thinking—it is a cognitive process that can be strengthened through learning and practice. According to C. R. Snyder's (1994) theory of hope, this process centers around the pursuit of goals and the belief that one is capable of achieving them. Young adolescents who experience difficulties that result in toxic stress may have a hard time envisioning a positive future for themselves. By recognizing and nurturing their unique talents and showing that you believe in their potential, you can foster their sense of hope by helping them picture a future where they can thrive. Consider the following ways to communicate hope to students:

- Envisioning language helps students picture their own future successes, which is the first step toward achieving positive outcomes. These successes may be large and in the distant future, such as a career goal, or smaller and more immediate, such as a classroom project due the following week. Either way, envisioning language helps students name positive identities and outcomes to increase confidence, aim high, and meet their goals.

- Offer teacher-guided choices about what to learn, how to learn it, or both. Doing so empowers students to become more invested in what they're learning and create their own vision for their academic future.

- Guide students in setting short- and long-term goals, breaking them into manageable steps, and developing the skills to meet them.

- Promote positive risk-taking, and reinforce that mistakes are part of learning.

- Use fictional stories or those about real people as a springboard for talking about successful scientists, writers, musicians, doctors, and other professionals, including specific role models that students identify. Discuss why students look up to their role models and the challenges those role models faced on the road to achieving their goals.

- Encourage students to see themselves as valuable members of the classroom community by giving them leadership roles.

- Talk to students about ways to find friends who believe in them and with whom they have an authentic connection.

- Help all students celebrate their accomplishments and the things that make them unique.

6. Foster Your Own Self-Care and Build a Supportive Community

Students who are experiencing toxic stress may need a higher than average amount of support, and we may also share in their emotional burden when we empathize with the challenges they face. Here are some ideas to help you take care of yourself and find the support you need:

- Pay attention to your emotional health. Learn and practice self-soothing strategies like deep breathing to help you calm down. Also, consider seeking out a therapist or counselor who can give you a safe, nonjudgmental space to vent and talk honestly about your experiences. If you have undergone trauma in your own life, you may feel especially stressed by seeing what students are going through. Remember to be patient with yourself just as you would with the students you teach, and seek out the help you need.

- Maintain good habits for your physical health, such as eating well, drinking enough water, exercising, and getting adequate sleep.

- Celebrate your own successes, large and small. Keep a list of accomplishments you feel good about to refer to on difficult days. Complimenting colleagues about what they're doing well can also help you stay in a positive mindset and build a sense of community.

- Think about how you can make your classroom space more welcoming, not just to students but to yourself as well. Do you have a comfortable chair? Does the room's décor reflect your personality?

- Find ways to keep a positive outlook. Think back on why you became a teacher in the first place, and think about others who inspire you, too.

- Maintain a healthy work-life balance that includes time for hobbies, relaxation, and family and friends.

Reference

Snyder, C. R. 1994. *The Psychology of Hope: You Can Get There From Here.* New York: Free Press.

Week Four

*As soon as I accomplish one thing, I just set a higher goal.
That's how I've gotten to where I am.*

—Beyoncé, singer-songwriter

Week four is a pivotal time for you as a teacher, for the classroom learning community you're creating with students, and for the developing healthy school culture as a whole. Now is a good time to pause and reflect on the significant work you've done in the last three weeks. You've worked to create conditions for academic, social, and behavioral success; foster positive teacher-to-student and student-to-student relationships; and establish a culture in which all students feel a sense of belonging and can picture themselves as contributing, responsible, and capable learners.

Goals for Week Four

This week focuses on assessing progress and planning ways to sustain the successes you've achieved so far. This assessment includes both the classroom community as a whole and students' individual progress toward their SMART goals. The week four goals also look at ways to successfully move forward by pinpointing areas for improvement and finding ways to stay energized throughout the year.

1. **Assess the classroom culture.** You've spent the first three weeks of school building community with students and creating a classroom culture in which all students can do their best learning. Now's the time to assess those efforts, celebrate successes, identify areas that still need work, and make a plan to continue strengthening this community.

2. **Have students assess their progress toward their academic goals.** An essential part of goal-setting is measuring and reflecting on progress. This week, students can review the SMART goals they set in week one, assess their progress toward meeting those goals, recalibrate their efforts as needed, and think about next steps if they've already met their goals.

3. **Establish proactive teacher-care routines.** As the school year progresses, it's important to keep self-care routines going strong. Now is a good time to take stock of your stress level, what's working well to help you maintain balance, areas that need improvement, and what strategies you may want to try going forward. This is also a good time to check in with your colleagues and share ways you can treat yourself and other teachers with compassion; improve your resiliency, optimism, and commitment to the profession; and celebrate professional progress and achievements.

Creating Conditions for Success

As you assess students' progress and your own self-care practices this week, give yourself credit for the hard work you've done so far this year. While we can always improve on our efforts, don't forget to look at what you've done that's worked well. Consider writing down a list of proud moments you've experienced so far this year: successful student collaborations, academic breakthroughs, moments of personal connection, or any other occasions that have brought you joy. Keep your list handy for times when you need a confidence boost as the year goes on.

Building Community

Use week four as an opportunity to take stock of the progress you've made in using *Responsive Classroom* practices to create a positive learning environment and a healthy classroom community. Think about the ways in which high-quality teaching and learning are defining characteristics of your work in each of the four domains: engaging academics, positive community, effective management, and developmentally responsive teaching. This is a reflection you should come back to regularly throughout the year so that you and the students you teach can continue to grow together.

Consider the measurements of progress in the following chart to help you assess the climate of your classroom based on the four domains.

Assessing Your Classroom Community

Domain	Measurements of Progress
Engaging Academics	• Students have opportunities to practice with coaching. • Students put content in their own words and assess their understanding through reflection. • Active teaching and interactive learning structures are used routinely.
Positive Community	• Students have learned each other's names and can work together productively. • Students have gone through the process of becoming invested in the rules.
Effective Management	• Students are knowledgeable about procedures and routines. • Clear and explicit directions set students up for success in all tasks. • Logical consequences are used regularly and consistently for all students.
Developmentally Responsive Teaching	• Responsive Advisory Meeting plans are designed purposefully to build students' positive relationships with peers and adults at school. • Brain breaks are used appropriately to help students refocus and recharge.

Responsive Advisory Meeting

This week, use your Advisory time to help students take stock of the progress they've made toward reaching their SMART goals and building a positive classroom culture. Continue to emphasize the act of reflection as an essential part of the learning process, not just within individual lessons but on a holistic level as well.

Arrival Welcome

Stand at the door and welcome students by name as they enter. Encourage students to take a moment to make sure their binders are organized as they get settled in their seats.

Announcements

Good Morning, Advisory Team!

A few weeks ago, you set SMART goals for yourself. Now is a good time to review those goals and do a self-check on your progress. Take out your SMART goal sheet and read through it. Write down one step you could take this week to help you meet one or more of your goals. Be ready to share.

Acknowledgments

Hand Up, Pair Up: Students walk around the room with one hand up. When they find a partner, they high-five, greet each other by name, and share their goal and their answer to the announcements prompt. When they finish, they raise their hand again and find a new partner. Repeat for 3–4 rounds.

Activity

Fact or Fiction: On an index card, students list three statements about themselves: two factual (true) and one fictional (false). For example:

- I have three brothers. [T]
- I used to live in Minnesota. [F]
- I was interviewed on television once. [T]

One student begins by reading their three statements to the class, and the class votes on which statement they think is fiction through a show of hands. The student who read reveals the false statement, then another student takes a turn. Continue until everyone has shared, or spread this activity over several Advisory meetings.

To close the meeting, ask students a reflection question: "What are some ways you can work with your classmates as the year goes on to help everyone meet their goals?"

Download a printable Responsive Advisory Meeting Planning Guide at https://www.responsiveclassroom.org/printables/.

Transitions and Nonclassroom Spaces

By the fourth week of school, most students are comfortable finding their way to and from classes, and they may be more relaxed about pausing in the hallway to socialize with their peers. While it's important to maintain a friendly atmosphere where students greet each other in the halls, too much time spent chatting can prevent students from getting to class on time. Teachers should be proactive about working with students to keep social time brief and get to class on time and focused. Use the following ideas to help students plan during Advisory, closing the day, or brief discussions during class:

- Brainstorm alternate opportunities during the school day to socialize with peers

- Lead students in conversations about the skills they are learning in class and how those skills can help them between classes as well

- Invite students to share ways they organize their lockers that help them find materials quickly

You can also use envisioning language to communicate expectations and encourage success related to transitions. For example:

- "I'm looking forward to seeing everyone first thing tomorrow and getting class off to a great start."

- "What would it look like to have your locker organized? How will that help you keep on schedule?"

- "What are some ways to help each other get to class on time when everyone's in the hallway?"

Closing the School Day

Closing the day during week four is a particularly valuable opportunity for students to evaluate how they are progressing academically, socially, and behaviorally, both in and outside the classroom. By this time, you may have used a variety of strategies to close the day, and you may prefer certain activities over others. Feel free to continue using activities that are working well with your classes. Whatever activities you choose, check in with your teammates or other colleagues to make sure that students are experiencing consistent practices and expectations in their different classrooms.

This week, consider the following reflection questions for use during closing the day activities or discussions:

- What are some strategies that have helped you make progress toward your goals so far this year?

- What are some obstacles you're facing as you work toward your goals? How can you find the support you need to overcome those obstacles?

- In what ways have you seen your classmates demonstrate empathy toward one another?

- What are some strategies you've used to help you manage anger or frustration?

- What are some ways to continue building a positive classroom and school culture?

- In what ways would you like to see our community improve?

- What about our classroom culture has had special meaning for you?

- What challenges might we have with keeping our classroom culture positive, and how might we deal with them?

Working With Your Team

Now that you're well into the school year, think about ways to keep academics exciting, maintain an energized and positive learning community, and help students who need additional assistance. Here are some ideas you might discuss with your team this week:

- Consider co-teaching a lesson or a unit with a teacher from a different subject. For example, an art teacher and a social studies teacher could co-teach a lesson about paintings from a specific historical period. Co-teaching across subjects helps students gain a deeper understanding of both areas and see how subjects interconnect in school and in the world at large.

- Select themes that can be incorporated across all subject areas on the team. This strategy also helps students see connections between subjects, and it can help build a sense of team identity and pride.

- Discuss strategies for creating a remediation schedule for any students who need additional support. Also, make a plan designating which teachers will be able to assist with each subject in preparation for finals or standardized testing.

- Plan a celebration for students. Identify academic behaviors students are successfully demonstrating as a team. Consider using pep rallies not just for athletic events but for celebrating accomplishments made on benchmark testing or for getting students energized in preparation for testing.

Maintaining Teacher Self-Care and Avoiding Burnout

Take week four to establish, schedule, and commit to a routine of self-care activities that you do alone or with other educators in your school. Self-care is critical to staying inspired, optimistic, and energized; to fueling your sense of efficacy so that you are able to bring your best to teaching; and to creating conditions in which students can succeed.

Teaching can take up much of your time and mental energy, but make sure to make time for your outside-of-work hobbies, relationships, and talents. Doing so can help you gain perspective and restore yourself emotionally so that you're able to feel more balanced and centered in your teaching and in the rest of your life. This also helps you show students what a healthy and well-balanced adult life looks like.

Setting Goals for Self-Care

Consider setting a SMART goal related to self-care to help you make and monitor progress. Here are some examples of the types of goals you might set.

Intellectual Growth

- This month, I'll try a new hobby I've been interested in.
- This year, I will read five books for pleasure.
- I will take a class this semester on a topic of personal interest.

Spiritual Growth

- This month, I will spend ten minutes a day journaling.
- I will learn meditation strategies this semester and practice them three times per week.
- This year, I will take a walk in the woods once a week to unwind.

Emotional Growth

- This semester, I will make time to call my sister once a week to catch up.
- I will work with a therapist this year to develop strategies for managing my stress and dealing with my emotions.
- This month, I will practice using reinforcing language in my relationships with my loved ones to help make those relationships stronger.

As you work toward each goal, reflect on the following questions:

- What do I need to do to make this behavior a routine?
- How is regularly doing this contributing to my growth?
- How is this helping me stay energized and focused as an educator?
- What obstacles am I facing, and how can I better address them?

 Download a printable SMART goal planner template at https://www.responsiveclassroom.org/printables/.

In addition to setting your own self-care goals, think about ways you can come together with your colleagues to build a stronger sense of community among the educators at your school. The basic human needs of belonging, significance, and fun are as important to adults as they are to young adolescents. Consider doing one or more of the following activities with your teammates or other professionals in your school:

- Each person brings a picture or some other nonverbal representation of their interests or identity to share.

- Each person shares one or two things about growing up in their home town that has had a positive impact on who they are today.

- Each person brings in an object or a picture that represents why they decided to become a teacher. Place the items in the center of the room and have people guess which item goes with each teacher. Debrief by having each person share which item is theirs and why that item represents their inspiration to be a teacher.

- Use the following questions to help your group explore what people have in common. First, answer the questions individually, then reconvene and compare answers to discover commonalities with your colleagues. Use these commonalities as conversation starters.

  - What is your favorite subject to teach?

  - What types of books do you like to read?

  - What animal are you most fond of?

  - What season do you like most?

  - What is your favorite television program?

  - What is the last movie you saw?

  - What type of music do you listen to most?

  - Where do you like to shop?

  - What is your favorite sports team?

  - What is your dream vacation?

Teaching Academics

This week, focus on assessing students' content knowledge and academic skills. Also take time to think about how the learning community is coming together. By this point in the school year, students are most likely working comfortably with partners or in small groups. If you see students working with the same friends all the time, think about having a more active hand in mixing up the groups so that students are working with a wider range of classmates.

Think back on the interactive learning structures and brain breaks you've tried so far this year. Which ones have worked well? How might you repeat class favorites but at an increased risk level? Try using interactive learning structures with more complicated academic content or asking for student volunteers to lead brain break activities.

Teaching Your Content

Week four is a good time to assess the progress students have made so far this year. Consider writing down the name of each student in a given class on a sheet of paper. Think about which students are progressing as expected and which ones need additional support. Write out your thoughts about what you could do to help each student advance. Make sure to include all students in this assessment; even those who are doing well in the class need to be challenged, so think of ways you can help them take their studies to the next level.

To keep students engaged as the school year goes on, make sure to keep referring back to students' goals. For example, after stating the learning objective for a new lesson, try giving students a moment to reflect on how what they're learning today could help them progress toward their SMART goals. This could simply be a quiet moment to think, or you could have students write a sentence or paragraph about this connection.

Planning Learning Objectives

Now that you've introduced active teaching, it's a good time to review your learning objectives to make sure they're adequately challenging to students. According to Marzano and Kendall's *New Taxonomy* (2007), there are six levels of cognitive processes:

1. **Retrieval**—The ability to recall and recognize information and to complete procedures or drafts without major errors

2. **Comprehension**—The ability to summarize, symbolize, and describe relationships between elements of knowledge

3. **Analysis**—The ability to classify information, to predict outcomes, to draw conclusions, and to critique and revise

4. **Knowledge utilization**—The ability to experiment, investigate, adapt, and make and defend decisions

5. **Metacognition**—The ability to set specific goals, self-assess knowledge and monitor progress, and determine the accuracy of one's own understanding

6. **Self-system thinking**—The ability to identify emotional responses to a piece of knowledge and why one has those associations, examine one's own level of belief that they can improve their understanding, and examine one's motivation to improve their understanding

Consider whether your learning objectives reflect enough of these higher levels of thinking to challenge students. The following chart offers examples of lower- and higher-level learning objectives in several subject areas.

Lower- and Higher-Level Learning Objectives

Subject	Lower-level thinking	Higher-level thinking
Science	The student can list the properties of an unknown white powder.	The student can investigate the properties of an unknown white powder and match it with one of the known substances.
Math	The student can write binomials.	The student can multiply binomials.
Language arts	The student can summarize a short story.	The student can develop and defend an argument about a short story.

Through active teaching, you can encourage students' progression from lower-order thinking skills to higher-order thinking skills. As you use envisioning language to coach students to higher achievement, they will feel supported and grow in academic confidence.

Interactive Learning Structures

Keep challenging students to take on higher-risk activities as the year goes on. This week, you might try a whole-class interactive learning structure, such as the following.

One-Sentence/One-Word Summaries

1. Name the learning goal. For example: "You're going to wrap up our unit on pottery making by writing a summary sentence. Then, as a class, we'll choose one word that captures that learning."

2. Give students 2–3 minutes to come up with one sentence that summarizes their new knowledge. A student might write: "Pottery is the art of making vessels out of clay by spinning it on a wheel, putting slabs together, or pinching it into shape."

3. Signal when time is up. Go around the room and have each student read their sentence. Clarify any misconceptions and reinforce their efforts: "Your summaries are very thorough and show you understand the different techniques you've studied."

4. After everyone shares, guide the whole class to collaborate on choosing one word—for example, "vessels"—that captures the essence of all the summary sentences.

This activity can also be done in small groups. Designate a recorder and a presenter for each small group. Give each group a few minutes to come up with a sentence together, then have each presenter share it with the rest of the class. The class then works together to choose one word, as described in step 4.

Brain Breaks

As the school year progresses, you may find it helpful to incorporate academic content into your brain breaks. This strategy can be especially helpful after an intense lesson or when students are preparing for tests. Try these two ideas for helping students remember key points about what they're learning.

Refocusing Brain Break: Metaphorical Connections

1. Students stand by their desks, perform a few simple movements (stretching, jogging in place), and then sit down.

2. The leader holds up an object and asks how it might relate to academic content. For example: "How is a ruler a metaphor for writing essays?"

3. Students have a minute or so to think about possible connections and then generate a metaphor.

4. The leader says "Time" and calls on students as they raise their hands. Metaphors may be serious or silly. For example:

   - Essays are divided into sentences and paragraphs, and rulers are divided into inches and fractions of inches.

   - Essays have to follow the "rules" of grammar.

   - Writing essays helps us measure our knowledge.

5. Repeat with a new object and question as time allows.

Recharging Brain Break: And Don't You Forget It!

1. Students stand at their desks or in a circle.

2. Choose a topic. For example: "Types of biomes." Give students a moment to think of their response (a phrase or word related to the topic).

3. As quickly as possible, the first student turns to the next person and says, "I say 'tropical rain forest,' and don't you forget it!"

4. The second student quickly turns to the next person and says, "Mariana said 'tropical rain forest,' I say 'savanna,' and don't you forget it!"

5. The third student quickly turns to the next person and says, "Ty said 'savanna,' I say 'tundra,' and don't you forget it!"

6. Continue briskly around the room until everyone has had a turn or time is up.

Teaching Discipline

As the year progresses, it's helpful to keep in mind that the mood of the classroom is deeply influenced by your demeanor. Staying firm, kind, and upbeat can set a positive mood that helps minimize misbehavior. Also, remember that you are a powerful model for students, and they are watching how you handle distractions, deadlines, and unexpected incidents throughout the day.

Effective Management

This week, think about the community behaviors you expect to see students successfully demonstrating, such as knowing each other's names, participating in group activities, and welcoming peers into conversations. If you observe the class having difficulty with one or more of these behaviors, now is a good time to reinforce expectations. Using Interactive Modeling to demonstrate the behavior again and creating an anchor chart with students may both be helpful.

For example, if you see that students are still struggling with entering the classroom respectfully, tell them what you're seeing in a calm, neutral way: "I'm noticing that often, when students are entering the room, people are pushing past each other and aren't paying attention to where they're going, so sometimes there are collisions and people get angry. We all need reminders sometimes when we're learning something new, so I'm going to model the expectations for entering the room to help you remember." After completing this Interactive Modeling, title a chart "Entering the Classroom Respectfully" with column titles "Looks like," "Sounds like," and "Feels like." Ask for student responses as you fill in those columns. Students might say that entering the classroom respectfully looks like "Making eye contact" or "Watching where you're going," that it sounds like "Mostly quiet with friendly greetings," and that it feels like "Calm" and "Focused." Refer to these characteristics in reinforcing language when you see students demonstrating the behavior going forward.

Working With the Rules

This week, pay attention to how well students are following the rules and what is helping them do so. Misbehaviors will still happen, but maintaining strong relationships with students, using effective teacher language, and clearly teaching and modeling expectations can help decrease them. These strategies will allow you to sustain a positive learning environment if they are consistently practiced throughout the school year. Each group of students has its own strengths and challenges, and students will show you the areas where they need additional practice or guidance. As these moments arise, encourage yourself to think of them as opportunities for you to give students what they need in order to be successful.

As students make progress toward reaching the SMART goals they set in week one, give them opportunities to check in on what learning strategies are working or not working for them. This reflection will help them get to know themselves as learners and take initiative in their own learning process. They can use a SMART Goal Self-Assessment chart to help them assess where they are in meeting their goals and what steps they can take to get the rest of the way there.

As students begin meeting the initial goals they set, guide them in creating new SMART goals. Remind them that their short- and medium-term SMART goals can be steps toward their long-term goals for their careers and their other future plans and dreams.

 Download a printable SMART Goal Self-Assessment chart template at https://www.responsiveclassroom.org/printables/.

Responding to Misbehavior

Continue to respond to misbehavior with empathy, staying kind yet firm as you stand by the expectations you've set for students. Take stock of which strategies work best with particular students, and look for ways to head off predictable patterns of misbehavior before they start. For example, two friends who tend to get rowdy together might be better off assigned to different groups during more energetic activities. Or, a student who is quick to anger might start drumming their fingers on the desk just before an outburst, signaling to you that this student needs to take Space and Time or go for a quick walk before things escalate. As the year goes on and you come to know students better, you will be more equipped to help them stay on task with the important business of middle school learning.

Reference

Marzano, Robert J., and John S. Kendall. 2007. *The New Taxonomy of Educational Objectives.* Thousand Oaks, CA: Corwin Press.

Further Resources

All the practices recommended in this book come from or are consistent with the *Responsive Classroom* approach to teaching—an evidence-based education approach associated with greater teacher effectiveness, higher student achievement, and improved school climate. *Responsive Classroom* practices help educators build competencies in four interrelated domains: engaging academics, positive community, effective management, and developmentally responsive teaching. To learn more, see the following resources published by Center for Responsive Schools and available at www.responsiveclassroom.org.

Middle School Motivators: 22 Interactive Learning Structures (from *Responsive Classroom*, 2016). These easy-to-use structures encourage all students to give their best effort, focus on learning goals, and collaborate effectively with one another in dynamic, purposeful, and respectful ways.

The Power of Our Words for Middle School: Teacher Language That Helps Students Learn (from *Responsive Classroom*, 2016). Practical information, tips, and examples for improving the professional language you use with students. Through your use of words and tone, you can more fully engage students in their learning and support positive development in all areas of their lives.

Refocus and Recharge: 50 Brain Breaks for Middle Schoolers (from *Responsive Classroom*, 2016). Quick, easy-to-learn activities that give students much-needed mental and physical breaks from rigorous learning, and increase their ability to stay on task and focus on the content you teach.

The Responsive Advisory Meeting Book: 150+ Purposeful Plans for Middle School (from *Responsive Classroom*, 2018). Use the combination of structure, purpose, and planning in this book to strengthen and enrich your Advisory meetings, providing students with a safe place to build respectful, trusting relationships with peers and adults, explore their interests, and develop new skills.

Seeing the Good in Students: A Guide to Classroom Discipline in Middle School (from *Responsive Classroom* with Rashid Abdus-Salaam, Andy Moral, and Kathleen Wylie, 2019). Learn how to tap into young adolescents' desire for autonomy in order to help them become self-motivated to behave in productive and positive ways—to benefit themselves, their peers, and the greater school community.

Yardsticks: Child and Adolescent Development Ages 4–14, 4th edition (by Chip Wood, 2017). This accessible reference concisely charts children's development, shows what behavior you can expect to see in the classroom (and at home) at different ages, and outlines ways you can support students' social-emotional and academic learning and growth.

Yardsticks Guide Series: Common Developmental Characteristics in the Classroom and at Home, Grades K–8 (from *Responsive Classroom*, 2018; based on *Yardsticks* by Chip Wood). Common characteristics of children's development are summarized in easy-to-scan, grade-specific guides for educators and parents.

Publisher's Acknowledgments

Center for Responsive Schools wishes to thank Ellie Cornecelli and Amber Searles for contributing their ideas and expertise to this book. Thanks also to the teachers and students of the schools that participated in the 2017 research study on practices for the first four weeks of school done by Center for Responsive Schools in partnership with Analytica, Inc. The time and effort invested by those schools and the feedback they provided helped us shape this content.

We hope this book will be a useful resource to middle school teachers in all subject areas who devote time and energy to helping students succeed. It is intended to make classroom management easier and to help you build a strong and healthy school community where students feel a sense of belonging and where learning can thrive. Whether you seek to capture and nurture the energy students bring with them at the beginning of the year or you want to bring a spark of new life to the classroom at other points in the year, we hope this book will help you meet your goals.

About the Contributors

Ellie Cornecelli is a Program Developer at Center for Responsive Schools. She began her career teaching in the classroom and developing curricula in the Washington, DC, metro area, where she began practicing the *Responsive Classroom* approach thirteen years ago. She believes deeply in student-centered instruction and fostering students' social-emotional growth to prepare them to be contributing innovators of the future.

Amber Searles is a Curriculum and Instructional Designer for Center for Responsive Schools, where she creates workshops and resources to support middle school educators in the *Responsive Classroom* approach. Amber was a *Responsive Classroom* practitioner in her middle school classroom in South Carolina for four years. The approach provided a strong framework for her instruction, and she saw how it set her students up for success in and out of the classroom.

Index

About the Publisher

Center for Responsive Schools, Inc., a not-for-profit educational organization, is the developer of *Responsive Classroom*®, an evidence-based education approach associated with greater teacher effectiveness, higher student achievement, and improved school climate. *Responsive Classroom* practices help educators build competencies in four interrelated domains: engaging academics, positive community, effective management, and developmentally responsive teaching. We offer the following resources for educators:

Professional Development Services

- Workshops for K–8 educators (locations around the country and internationally)
- On-site consulting services to support implementation
- Resources for site-based study
- Annual conferences for K–8 educators

Publications and Resources

- Books on a wide variety of *Responsive Classroom* topics
- Free monthly newsletter
- Extensive library of free articles on our website

For details, contact:

Center for Responsive Schools, Inc.
85 Avenue A, P.O. Box 718
Turners Falls, Massachusetts 01376-0718

800-360-6332   www.responsiveclassroom.org
info@responsiveclassroom.org